Dear Susan—
We believe in you!
— WITH LOVE!
Juel + Mollie

INFINITE
LOVE&MONEY

INFINITE
LOVE&MONEY

Find Balance, Love, and
Financial Freedom with this
Practical Guide for Couples

MOLLIE & JOEL
SINGH SALOMON

Acknowledgements

We would like to thank the following people:

Glenn – For all of your love and support, we are forever grateful. (From Mollie to Glenn, I am me, because we are we).

Tara – For the 17 reasons you already know.

Miriam – We are grateful for your support, encouragement and wisdom.

Mike Dooley – We met because of you...none of this would be possible without your infinite wisdom, love, and support.

Andy Dooley – We are eternally grateful for your generous spirit and constant reminder to keep our vibes high. As you always say, "Feeling first, manifestation second."

Laura Hughes, Terri Liggins, and Brenda Nagle – Thank you for your feedback and edits.

Rob & Beth Davidsen, Sean Ryan & Ada Lee, Tom Abrams, Lisa Beichl, Peter Sharkey & Karen McNiven, Andrea Beenham, Ken Kim, and Chara Rodriguera – We really appreciate you for your emotional support, the detailed comments and insightful thoughts when you read our first draft.

Foreword

Is it possible to have both love and money in infinite supply?

As a finance professional and Law of Attraction mindset coach, I know this to be true:

ALL your dreams can come true – whether financial, romantic, or otherwise.

In my money mindset & manifesting work with entrepreneurial women we focus on combining the magical with the practical. Students learn how to start taking confident control of their money to make it work for them, while shifting old belief systems and limiting beliefs to transform their actual relationship with money.

It's usually not far into this process that students start to talk about their other significant relationship...that with their partner.

Conversations around money with partners can be difficult and downright stressful. My students often wonder how they can create true financial security and freedom for themselves when their partner is in a very different headspace...or has very different financial habits.

So imagine how thrilled I was to see Mollie and Joel come together to write this book!

Mollie and Joel have merged their expertise on relationships and finances to help couples put aside their limiting beliefs and use the Law of Attraction so that they can manifest BOTH *Infinite Love and Money.*

Their approach is perfectly in sync with the advice I give my students, "You have to fit your own oxygen mask first."

Through this book, you will get to first understand yourself as an individual – what your money personality is, and then why it is. You will not only be asked to draw on the memories behind your financial personalities, you'll also be given the tools to accept and adjust old attitudes to improve your own money relationship.

You will learn about differences in money personalities and how to handle conflict and resolve those awful financial arguments.

Joel's financial knowhow combined with Mollie's relationship expertise will help facilitate your understanding of both.

The book weaves a very relatable parable of a couple's financial and relationship troubles – demonstrating the challenges that this toxic mixture can create.

We get to learn from this couple's mistakes and see how better communication and the practical application of the strategies in this book would have resulted in a very different outcome.

The lessons and exercises in this book will empower you to dig deeper and fly higher.

This book is sure to bring you closer to financial freedom and to loving your life – and your partner – even more!

MIRIAM CASTILLA
The Effectologist
Money & Mindset Mentor to Women in Business
Author of Today's Woman – Life Balance Secrets

Dear Couple,

Welcome to your financially free future! We are excited to be on this journey with you. We recognize that this will be a process, and we celebrate you and your willingness to do this work together.

This book is designed to honor you as individuals that come from different backgrounds and perspectives. You will turn toward each other, connecting more closely, by finding a deeper understanding of each others' history and belief systems. This connection allows your bond to grow stronger as you learn to make decisions together.

Our deepest hope is that you learn more about each other, valuable financial lessons included in this book, and how to discuss and grow your finances together. We want you to be in a better situation than you are now. We do know that nothing will change if we change nothing.

Again, thank you for allowing us to be a part of your journey.

We believe in you!

With infinite love!

Joel and Mollie

Joel: Joel@SaLaurMor.com

Mollie: Mollie@MollieSingh.com

Genesis of Infinite Love & Money

It was 7:22 a.m. on May 10th of 2018. I had just left Crawford Park on my normal jogging route. I was running up the 100 meter hill past the Korean War Veterans Memorial around the beautiful rose garden through the "forest." As I went down the path to Lincoln Avenue and then back up again toward Ridge Street, I made my way out of the park. I had just entered Betsy Brown Road when the idea hit me: Mollie and I should work together!

We had met a few months earlier at Mike and Andy Dooley's Train the Trainer Conference for Infinite Possibilities™ (IP™) in New Orleans. We had both been certified in Santa Fe in 2017, but neither of us had the chance to get to know each other until New Orleans. We were both guest speakers at that conference. Mollie had talked about how she was starting a coaching practice for couples that combined the teachings of Infinite Possibilities™ and the Gottman 7 Principles™.

I'm not sure why it took me two months to have that "aha" moment, though it must have been percolating for some time. On my run, it finally hit me, "Isn't money one of the main reasons why relationships fail???"

What do you and your partner disagree about most often? If money was not one of the top two reasons you stated, congratulations, because you are in the minority. Finances are what couples, married or otherwise, tend to fight about the most. We find more people are wondering why personal finance and personal relations is not a part of the high school curriculum.

I actually knew the issue, and as I made the turn on North Ridge Street, the idea became more fleshed out. Mollie and I *needed* to work together. Why not do a seminar or webinar together? Wait! Why not write a book together?

So, we decided to combine the concepts of Infinite Possibilities™ we had been teaching to our individual clients and our respective specialties – me regarding prosperity and Mollie regarding love. I have the expertise of decades in the financial industry, and Mollie is a thriving couples' coach and a Gottman Seven Principles Leader™.

I had started down this path because I was thinking about my meeting with one of my new prosperity clients in Manhattan. He and I had spent the last few weeks shifting his negative thoughts about himself and the likelihood of him ever getting to work at his dream job. But his cashflow and budgeting issues kept on coming up. We decided to spend a session playing the Budget Game (Where is Your Cash Going? – Chapter 15) to see where their cash was really going.

The prior week, I had told him that this would be a perfect time to get his wife involved in our process. He explained that his wife does not concern herself in this aspect of their relationship. He said "I'm the money guy and she doesn't ask questions. She knows I have this handled!" *Oh really*, I thought to myself. And then, of course, I realized this is how most couples do it. One of the two partners handles things without communicating the whole picture to the other. This can't work well!

I thought back to my last marriage and we had an agreement to discuss all purchases over $500, unless, of course, we were buying each other a surprise weekend getaway. We were definitely on the same page regarding money. We loved to spend money...on experiences. We didn't have a limit on our travel budget, but neither of us wasted money frivolously. I always felt we had the right balance of enjoying life and being frugal. And our communication was wide open.

This clearly wasn't the case with my new client. And as I jogged from North Ridge Street to Argyle Road, I realized I ran into a huge need for the world: better money discussions between couples! A way to communicate about money, discover each other's subconscious beliefs, and understand why each person in the relationship is acting the way they are – because of their money upbringing and their subsequent fears about money.

I had already started the research for my second book and so the idea continued to percolate over the coming months as I wrote the manuscript for *The 9 Money Rules Millionaires Use*.

Timing is everything, and Mollie and I crossed paths again through another group in 2019. It was there that I learned more about her work as a love coach. She was working with couples to help them create a deeper bond. She was helping them understand more about themselves as individuals, as well as each other. Ultimately, she was helping couples create deeper and stronger bonds. And while working with couples, she was penning her new Couples Workbook, *Infinitely Loving*. Combining our work proved to be a natural fit.

As 2019 progressed, we decided to combine our key concepts in a webinar. In fact, some of the key concepts in *Infinite Love* and Money came from a webinar we recorded in early 2020 in Manhattan. As we both learned more about our respective expertise and our philosophies of empowering our clients, we realized the synergies that existed between us and we needed to do more work together.

This book is intended for couples who want to improve their relationship and their relationship with money. It covers the history and background of your beliefs and emotions related to money and teaches you how to connect and turn toward your partner. It also walks through differences, especially money differences, between the two people in the relationship and how these differences can be celebrated. We also discuss key concepts in resolving conflict.

Each chapter goes through an anecdote and gives you the ability to do exercises to enhance your money learning experience.

Thank you again for reading this book. We are so excited to join you on your infinitely loving journey.

What You Will Experience

Welcome to your financially free and infinitely loving future! What? Money and love happily together? Yes! Joel and I are here to lead you through some deep emotional work to help you live your dream life and understand each other better.

Some of our chapters start with anecdotes. However, most chapters start with a parable about a couple going through a divorce. This story is about my ex–husband and me. Sadly, it is a true story – all of this happened during my relationship and during the mediation process for the divorce. When all was said and done, as we were walking out, my attorney handed me a pin that said, "Divorce is expensive, freedom is priceless."

Of course, at that time I chuckled.

Afterward, I wondered, what does freedom mean to me? To me, freedom is loving someone freely – and being loved freely – with financial security and without the threat of breaking up. So, how did I get to be truly free? Well, I studied relationships. I became a *Seven Principles Leader*™ taught by the renowned relationship experts, the Gottman's – Dr. John and Dr. Julie Gottman. Dr. John Gottman wrote the best–selling book, *The Seven Principles That Make A Relationship Work*. And they have their famous "Love Lab" in Seattle, Washington. Going on 40 years now, they have studied couples as a scientific experiment. They have observed and documented couples. They have also measured physiological responses in couples after conflict. Through this research, they have identified how the "masters" succeed and the "disasters" fail. From their work, they have identified how to create great, loving relationships. From them and their work,

I learned how to improve my relationships. And I used the lessons from Mike Dooley, author of the best–selling book *Infinite Possibilities: The Art of Living Your Dreams*™, to create my best life and find my greatest love. My freest love.

Today, Joel and I bring to you our stories, our lessons, and teach you the following:

- What your money personality types are;

- Your beliefs and your partners' beliefs about money, and where they come from;

- What role emotions play in your finances;

- How to harness your emotions and have them work *for* you, not against you;

- What are and what were your dreams and desires and how you can honor them today;

- Your differences, how to respect them, and how to recover from conflict. Spoiler alert: Conflict is not a bad thing. The magic is in the recovery;

- Credit scores – what are they and why they matter;

- Where your cash is going and later, your kid's money;

- Finally, your financial freedom.

We are happy to be on this journey with you and look forward to hearing from you.

If you like this book, please consider leaving us a review on Amazon. And if you want money coaching, love coaching or money and love coaching, please contact us.

We believe in you with love!

Our tips on the material

It is not lost on us that we have included a lot of information in this book. Our intention is to help you both get to know yourselves better, each other better, to love each other deeper because of it, and to be financially free. To that end, we suggest tackling one chapter a week. Though, if you need more time, you should discuss it with each other and create your plan to work through the book together.

The end of each chapter contains exercises that afford you the time to discuss the questions and content. We do ask you to reflect, dig deep into your individual backgrounds, and share with each other. We do realize that this can make some feel raw and exposed, however, it is intended to give you both the space to do so while offering your love the safety to do so. We will also have some Hot Hints, that serve as quick tips or take–aways.

Throughout the book, you will also notice we use terms such as "energy," and "flow." This is because we believe in the Law of Attraction – that what we think about, is what we bring about. We also believe that the world is abundant. While we understand that you must take steps toward your abundant life, your thoughts must lead the way. For abundance to flow into your life, you must allow that flow. In this book, we will touch upon ways to do so with intention.

And with that, we begin your journey to your infinitely loving and financially free future.

Table Of Contents

CHAPTER 1:
MONEY PERSONALITY TYPES

"I am here tonight to warn you that you have yet a chance and a hope of escaping my fate. You will be haunted by three spirits...Remember what has passed between us!"

These lines are from A Christmas Carol, a movie that has had more than twenty different remakes and originally adapted from Charles Dickens' 1843 classic of the same name. This quote comes from the spirit of Ebenezer Scrooge's partner, Jacob Marley, who led the same lifestyle as Scrooge did up to that point: a life whose sole purpose was the pursuit of money.

If you haven't watched one of the movies or read the book, we highly recommend watching since it is the ultimate financial transformation of a man. He pays his employees as little as possible, keeps as much as he can, and cares for no other human — not even his nephew and his family. He doesn't allow for "flow."

After the appearance of the three spirits — those of Christmas past, present, and future, Scrooge, the epitome of The Greedy Type (as described later in this chapter), transforms by spending the rest of his life doing good for others.

Ebenezer, while being a fictitious character, is a good example of how someone can change their money personality. In the end, Ebenezer found balance and as a result, happiness. If change, or more specifically, balance is what you desire, we are here to help you find it.

Knowing your money personality type gives you the opportunity to know yourself better and adjust as needed. Even Ebenezer was able to change. In Appendix 1, we have a survey that we encourage you to take. It will help you assess your money personality type. As you will see when you take the survey, and then re–take it over the coming weeks, you are not only one money personality type. You are a mixture of, at least a few, and those few can also change over time and in various situations. When you fill the survey out, don't dwell on the adjective, just fill it out based on what you are feeling right now. We encourage you to take this survey a few more times over the next several weeks, to see what it tells you.

Knowing your partner's personality type allows you insights into your partner's experiences and how those experiences shaped their mind and life. Your relationship takes deliberate effort, so as you read this chapter, remember to be gentle with yourself and your love. While it may feel scary to go this deep into your past and your feelings, these insights offer you the opportunity to open up and grow closer together..

Note: We believe your money personality type is fluid. It can change based on circumstances, or even with your partner, as a reaction to their money personality type. You may find that you spent more freely when you were single, but when partnered up, you pinch pennies. Somewhere in between those two seemingly disparate money types is who you really are. Some may even find that they have two competing money personality types. That is great! You have aspects of both traits that helps you balance your habits. The goal after all, is to find balance. It is likely that you have a primary and secondary money personality type. You may even have a third money personality type. These personality types are a part of you. As you read the Financial Backgrounds chapter (Chapter 2), you will uncover where your Money Personality Type was formed.

So, why change? If you strongly exhibit one of these personality types, it is likely that you do not have balance. Or you may find that many financial conflicts arise between you and your partner. Or you may just want to change your financial situation. Understanding your background will help you understand your own behavior better. Similarly, understanding each other's backgrounds will help you understand each other better. This understanding will help you change and build a stronger bond as you help each other

We do recommend starting with small changes. At the end of this chapter, we offer some concrete ways to make your changes. Be sure to be patient with each other as changes take time. We recommend committing to one small change every month, and reassessing as you move toward your financial freedom.

Please note that even the smallest of changes can have huge influences on your emotions, psyche and relationship. A change, any change, disrupts the pattern that you are in. That is what we are here to do – create new habits and patterns. As you do this, we highly recommend "knowing your why." As you start this financial journey, ask yourselves, "Why are we making this change?" Recall, we are here to teach you how to make yourselves financially free as soon as possible. And what is possible, is only what works for you both. The changes must be palatable to both of you. That way, your changes will take hold and will feel more like a "get to do," rather than a "have to do."

You should first acknowledge that a change is needed and that you both have a desire to work on the change because, well – you are here reading this book. Now decide on, what to change. And this may be controversial, but our recommendation would be that if there is massive stress attached with looking at your accounts – like fear or worry, then don't look. Not forever though. We suggest having one person do it. And maybe look at them together every couple of weeks. Work together towards a feeling of calm and ease and a knowing that everything will work out just fine.

So, what is your money personality type? First, it is important to realize that you and your partner may have different primary personality types. Or that you and your partner may share the same primary type, and yet have differing secondary personality types. This can cause conflicts – and that is ok. Please see the Recover and Resolve – Chapter 11 to help you through them. You should find a way to work together – toward the change you both want to see. Perhaps start with a monthly budget and a bi–monthly meeting to review your budget and your progress. Doing this together can help you both know you are on the same team and can also alleviate stress.

As you talk through your changes, remember to also consider what habits you want to keep. Do you want to save more? Great! Do you want to still splurge? That is great too! All we are recommending is to find balance with your partners' desires.

We know that no one changes in a day, but being self-aware of your money purchases is a good start to your transformation. Start tracking what you spend money on. The act of acknowledging everything will start your transformation. You will see small shifts that will ultimately lead to a change in your money personality type.

Take it slow. Know that there may be times when you revert to your prior ways. It is important to acknowledge those times with your partner. Being patient about these events will also ease the transition for you both.

As you learn about your own, and your partner's money personality traits, remember to be open, patient and supportive. If something goes wrong – if someone splurges too much, or if someone feels like they aren't saving enough – that is ok. Have the conversation with each other. Again, refer to Chapter 11 (Recover and Resolve) for a way to calmly discuss your feelings. Acknowledging yourself and your partner gives you both power. You are in a partnership, so best to find a solution that works for you both.

As you utilize the techniques in this book and begin to transform, your daily lives are likely to see less arguing and disagreements. Remember to track your successes. Success is important to acknowledge and celebrate.

Below you will find the seven Money Personality Types that we have created. You can remember the seven types with this acronym: SUGA' PIE.

The descriptors of the money personality types follow. Rest assured that while the names are provocative and one dimensional, each type has a positive aspect as well. The descriptions below offer the sharpest characteristics to help demonstrate each personality type.

Hot Hint! Change takes time. Please be patient with yourselves and each other as you make your transformations. These descriptors are not meant to be used for judgment or fuel for your fire when you are upset. And if one of you reverts back to prior habits, please take heart and discuss the issue openly with one another. Refer to Chapter 11 (Recover and Resolve) to help you discuss your challenges.

After you read through each type, consider:

- Which one or two personality types most closely resonate with *you*.

- Which one is your primary and which is your secondary personality type?

- Which one do you think your partner is?

Take some time to discuss your own personality type(s) with one another and what you see in each other. Allow your partner to identify their money personality type before suggesting what you think it is.

If you prefer to have some guidance on your Money Personality Type, we developed a survey in Appendix 1 to accurately assess which three traits are most prevalent since no one exhibits only one of them at all times. We use this survey with clients as it is oftentimes difficult to self–assess your own personality. We often resonate with more than one trait, or we do not realize that we are how we are. Mollie will attest to this! She often thinks she is far more conservative than she actually is. Perhaps try a self–evaluation as well as the survey?

Again, please remember to *not* use these terms as ammunition against each other. Rather, use the terms and the descriptions to help better understand yourself and your partner. Then consider, how that is serving or not serving you and your partner in your quest for financial freedom.

S stands for The Splurger Type

The Splurger Type regards money as infinite. They often believe money is endless. It is always coming and more will always come. Even when evidence points to the contrary.

Their mindset is: characterized by thoughts of entitlement. They may think or even say: "I deserve to spend my hard—earned cash on whatever I want!" Unfortunately, they don't take into consideration the impact their actions have on the couple's financial situation. They also don't realize they are likely the main source of their financial problems.

Their attitude is: one of desperation, which is what drives them to spend money. They tend to be swayed by emotions and impulses. They don't understand that what they do adversely affects their partner, even if they are making a purchase for their partner. Rather, they think that what they do with their money is more important — when they're spending it —than anything else. It's akin to an addiction where buying things is the only way to satisfy their addiction.

Their actions: include being swayed by a fancy display case at a storefront, or the newest fancy "toy" being advertised. And it becomes so desirable, that cost is inconsequential. Similarly, whims play a role and suddenly a momentary desire is a "must buy." They don't necessarily want the shiny object for themselves. They are just in it for the "thrill of the buy." It affects men and women alike – from fancy guitars, to pretty dresses or designer purses to shiny new cars. The Splurger Types are likely to go into debt for their splurges.

Search Engine Optimization (SEO) is the downfall for The Splurger Type. It is a built—in software tool used by websites from companies that enable searching on the internet, and it tracks (remembers) what you look at across devices. It remembers what you searched for and what you purchased. And, at the most inconvenient times, advertisements will pop up to lure you to make a purchase.

This behavior makes it challenging for The Splurger Type to handle money because they can't tell what's going to pop up that's going to make them want to spend money. When it comes to money, they live moment to moment rather than looking at the big picture of their life. They may have buyers remorse, but still not return the splurge.

The main reason to change from The Splurger Type is that you also want to save and invest your money so that you can enjoy it in the future too. The Splurger Types don't tend to have any money saved and, thus, are unlikely to be funding their retirement adequately. Thinking about the future as well as the present will serve them better.

It's important to understand that splurges will still happen even after you've consciously decided with your partner to change. Short of being visited by the ghost of Christmas–past, The Splurger Type won't become a saver overnight. Taking it slow and planning for the splurges is an important step in your change process.

The benefits are: The Splurger Types have an abundant mindset. They believe that money comes easily and frequently. The Splurger Types also make great gift givers. They can be generous to a fault and will often surprise people with gifts. The Splurger Types like to ride the wave. Like surfers who need to have a strong enough wave to ride, The Splurger Types don't want a really weak wave or a Tsunami. They have to ensure the flow is right and they allow money and prosperity to flow.

Our proposal: Plan for a monthly splurge. Perhaps have a monthly allowance just for your splurges. A bit of splurging is actually good as long as it is within your means. We want your cashflow to be positive every month. Your splurges can be a fun game to spend on something special once a month or every other month. Oftentimes allowing for an occasional splurge can even get you in the "Abundance Mindset." For example, allowing for a splurge of fancy jam or a special glass of wine with dinner will help remind you that abundance is inevitable.

A built–in splurge will allow for the Law of Attraction to be set into motion. It allows you to focus on the abundance and prosperity in your life. Not the scarcity or lack of it. And what you focus on, you attract.

U is for The Unconscious Type

The Unconscious Type tends to be willfully unaware (unconscious) about doctrines or theories. They often know enough about their finances to know that they are not where they want to be. In fact, it often pains them to have the full knowledge of their circumstances. Because they are unconscious, they are not always aware of their own financial wants or needs and therefore they tend to sacrifice them.

Their mindset is: characterized by a poverty mindset. They are afraid of what they may find, so they deliberately don't look at their accounts. They will never admit that they are afraid, and will act like everything is ok. They live in a dream state – often believing that everything will work out. And they do not want to be bothered by the details.

Their attitude is: one of unknowing. Typically, The Unconscious Types don't want to deal with the consequences of what they find in their finances. The Unconscious Types don't really have an attitude about money one way or another. Money comes and goes. They have enough in the moment or they don't. They will often be so unaware of what they have in the bank that they will overspend and rack up hundreds of dollars in overdraft fees – even if all they had to do was wait one more day to buy that present. They are that unaware of what their bank account looks like. This lack of awareness is also likely to put them in debt.

Their action: is lacking. The Unconscious Types don't have an action plan related to money. As far as their actions are concerned, they are unaware of steps to be taken and therefore only think day–to–day or moment–to–moment. This is the type of short–term thinking that makes it harder to take care of the future.

They do whatever is in front of them with no thought of how it's going to affect them later. You can't wake them up unless you first make them aware that there is a problem. Once they gain the awareness, they must want to find a way to change. And once that happens, we encourage lessons on money. Perhaps some one–on–one coaching with Joel and Mollie?

The benefits are: Unconscious types are protecting their feelings. They know that feelings and emotions including sadness, being over-whelmed, or anger do not serve them – or for that matter anyone. They subconsciously know that looking at their finances makes them feel awful. So, they stop. This can be beneficial because when you feel any emotion, you attract more of it into your life. So, if they think they are likely to feel any negative emotion regarding their financial situation, remaining unconscious to it will stop that emotion from perpetuating. That said, we don't recommend never looking at your accounts, but if they are creating a feeling of extreme sadness or de-pression then you don't need to look at them daily or even weekly.

Make a plan to look at them biweekly or monthly.

The main reason to change from an Unconscious Type is that you want to save and invest your money so that you can enjoy it in the future too.

Our Proposal: Acknowledge that at least one of you is an Uncon-scious Type. Start a conscious savings plan. Commit to looking at your accounts weekly.

G is for The Greedy Type

The Greedy Types have an excessive desire, especially for wealth or possessions. Unlike The Splurger Types, The Greedy Types are purposeful about the possessions they acquire. In their minds, it helps bring about status or feelings of wealth. Also, unlike The Splurger Types, they are not likely to be in debt.

Their mindset: is characterized by poverty mindset. This may seem counter–intuitive, but poverty is actually their motivation. More spe-cifically, the lack of poverty. Thus, their mind focuses on poverty. They are scared to do without. All that matters to them is money. They can't stand the thought of poverty and they will not be controlled by it. Ironically, this controls them. They think that anyone who puts up with poverty is lazy and deserves whatever they get because of it. They don't respect people whom they consider to be financially less–off than them.

Their attitude is: one of hoarding. Because of their poverty mind-set, they hoard their money. No matter how much of a return on their investment they make, they expect to make more. They are very up-set when their investments do not do as well as expected.

Their actions: include a heavy focus on managing their money; in fact, they negotiate harshly. This means that they have to win at all costs. The negotiation could be in a business arrangement or in de-ciding whether or not to buy a car or a house, and how much to pay for it.

The Greedy Type tends to be impulsive and adventurous. They are risk takers. But not with their money. With their money, they like to be in control. They tend to make a lot of money and not be very gen-erous.

The benefits are: Given that the definition of greed means an in-tense desire, one could see that as a positive. After all, The Greedy Type goes after money with gusto. It is their intense desire for money that helps them acquire it. In order to become financially free, you do need to have a strong desire.

So, why change from being The Greedy Type? Remember Eben-ezer Scrooge? What happened after he shifted his life's purpose from the pursuit of money to the caring about others and using money to save people? He was happier overall and became more fulfilled emotionally.

The main reason to change from being The Greedy Type is that you will feel better about yourself, you strengthen your relationship with your partner, and you improve your relationship with others. You will be no longer be hoarding money. You will be sharing it with others for the greater good. And, since you still have that great desire for money, you will have plenty for both of you.

11

Like Scrooge, maybe you can help someone in need. One of the best ways to serve yourself is to be in service of others.

<u>Our Proposal</u>: Consider focusing on other desires besides money. Maybe you have an intense desire for your relationship to be the best it can be. That balance will be helpful not only for your relationship, but also for your well–being.

A stands for The Accumulator Type

The Accumulator Type is known for saving and is reluctant to give or spend. The Accumulator Types tend to be hoarders and are not very generous. They differ from The Greedy Types in that they save their money. They don't invest any, like The Greedy Types do. The Greedy Types will do anything to be financially free, while The Accumulator Types only hoard.

<u>Their mindset</u>: is characterized by a strong need for safety and security, so much so, that they operate in a poverty mindset. They are generally risk–averse with their money. Unlike the greedy ones, they are far more conservative with their investments, if they invest at all. They celebrate the balance rather than the rate of return on their financial investments.

<u>Their attitude</u>: is generally negative. They have a worry mindset. They are always prepared for the inevitable doomsday. One of their main focuses is saving and making sure they never have to worry about money. Common thoughts tend to be: "we can't afford that! That is too expensive." This attitude may serve them adequately, but we believe that having an abundance mindset will serve them even better.

<u>Their actions</u>: include doing their best to include their partner in all their decisions around money and make their partner feel safe and secure about their financial future.

They tend to "save their money for a rainy day." It is good to plan for the future, but if you are always worried (we define that as "negative future planning") then you will keep your money in saving and checking accounts instead of having your money work for you (in investments). We recommend that instead of always worrying about the bad weather, to think about what you do want to happen; think about the bright sunny, cloudless days.

The benefits are: The Accumulator Type saves money and that's not a bad thing! Having more money in your accounts is good. When an emergency comes up, they will have plenty to cover those expenses. Another benefit of being an Accumulator Type is that they will learn about the various types of savings accounts that are prevalent in the world and can make informed decisions—as well as help others.

Our Proposal: Is being an Accumulator Type good or bad? Our answer is controversial: being only a saver is not good. This is also known as "hoarding" and in Joel's 2019 book, *The 9 Money Rules Millionaires Use*, he explains the importance of giving as one of the core nine money rules. If you are only hoarding, saving your money, and not giving some away or spending it on yourself or on others, you are not putting that money out into the world and it won't flow back to you in multiples of what you put out there. After all, we are looking at your cash flow. So, think about ways you can actually share your money with others. Do you have a favorite charity? Donate to them. Consider reviewing the attributes of The Splurger Type and acting like them once a month!

The main reason to change from being The pure Accumulator Type is similar to shifting from The Greedy Type, especially as you pursue giving and splurging: you will feel better about yourself, your relationship with your partner, and your relationship with all other humans. Instead of hoarding, you can share it with others for the greater good. You may want to take a percentage of each dollar or euro you earn and donate it to a charitable organization.

The reasons to shift from The pure Accumulator Type are two–fold.

First, you can just save without investing. For example, you can put your money in a regular savings account. However, the power of compounding interest does not work in your favor when you only do this. In 2021, the average savings account earned less than 1% in interest. However, if you invested the money, you could earn more. We do not recommend having all your money in savings accounts, earning less than 1%.

Second, you can save too much. If you are only spending on your own necessities (shelter, food, water, and the expenses associated with working) and then saving the rest, the flow of money is not happening. Rather, there is a stoppage that inhibits flow. We believe that it is no coincidence that it is called cash flow. Without sending it out into the world, it won't flow back to you for more enjoying, investing, and sharing. Further, money is energy. Wait, isn't money a physical thing? How can it be physical and non–physical? We believe that money contains the energy we, as a society, assign to it. When we think of money, hopefully, we think of it in positive terms. In this way, for positivity to come toward us, we must also offer it outward. This is the same for money.

P stands for The Protectionist Type

The Protectionist Types think that money is a rare commodity and they have to protect theirs. They're constantly worried about it and they know that unforeseen circumstances can destroy it in a nanosecond.

Their mindset is: characterized by fear. As the name indicates, The Protectionist Types are most concerned with protecting their money — at all times. They are in a constant state of worry about their money, about their job, and about the financial state of the country. They are more worried than savers. And as such, they are also in a poverty mindset. They tend to be the ones who have cash on hand – usually under their mattress, or in the freezer. For example, they will be able to tell you about the real estate crash of 2008/2009 in detail. They will also remember that stocks dropped 40 – 57% in 2008. However, they are not likely to also pontificate about the stock rebound that started in 2009.

Their attitude is one of anxiety. They are more than risk averse

— they are actually afraid of the past financial crashes. In fact, they think that something can go terribly wrong with their money at any time. They're not always very nice about it either, which puts a great burden on their partner and children to meet their beliefs and standards.

Their actions include: keeping all their money in cash. They are quick to say no to all financial decisions. They will often veto their partner when it comes to doing anything with their money other than saving it. They believe investments are far too risky.

The benefits are: The Protectionist Type has a low likelihood of ever losing money. If the stock market crashes or the real estate market collapses, their money won't be impacted.

The main reason to change from being The Protectionist Type is similar to shifting from The Accumulator Type money personality type, especially as you pursue giving and splurging: you will feel better about yourself and your relationship with your partner. Because you are allowing money to flow out into the world, it must come back to you. You will be no longer be protecting your money, and you will still have plenty. Instead, you will see that your money is actually there to protect you and your world. You will be sharing it with others for the greater good.

When an emergency comes up, The Protectionist Types tend to have plenty to cover those expenses. Don't let this fool you though. Yes, it is good to be prepared for that rainy day, but preparing for only rainy days is not beneficial to you, your partner, or your larger community.

Our Proposal: Our advice for The Protectionist Types is similar to what we say for The Accumulator Types. We ask that you think about ways you can share your money and be kinder with your partner about your worries. Do you have a favorite cause or charity? Consider starting by contributing some percentage of your earnings to it. What material item would really make you happy? Buy it! Or consider what would really make your partner happy and buy that! Remem-

15

ber, when you put that money out into the world, it will flow back to you; oftentimes multiples of what you put out there. So, think about ways you can actually share your money with others. Consider reviewing the attributes of The Splurger Type and acting like them once a month!

I stands for The Investor Type

The Investor Type is always looking for ways to make more money. They want their money to work for them. It could be via stocks, education or negotiating for better deals.

Their mindset is: characterized by getting the best deal. They are bargain hunters. They get excited to buy something for 80 cents if it is worth a dollar. They go beyond the "dollar saved is a dollar earned" mindset — to them, everything is an investment. They look at everything in terms of the resale amount, or rather, how much can their investment get them. They view everything as a negotiation, which can be off putting to those around them. Often, they can forget to enjoy the moment.

Their attitude: is one of self–assurance. They tend to be confident in their investments. They have researched their investments and believe that anything they go for is a sure bet. Recall that they are bargain hunters. So, they look for cheap investments that they believe will go up a lot.

Their actions: focus on making money. In fact, The Investor Type tends to spend money to make money. They don't want to miss out on any investment opportunities and would rather ask for forgiveness than ask for permission. They spend money to benefit their lives.

The Investor Type takes action by paying a lot of attention to the financial markets and worrying about the best way to make their assets grow in value. For example, they'll go into real estate and do their best to negotiate the price, then they will spend an inordinate amount of energy and money to raise the value of their property. Often not realizing that spending less would have yielded a better return.

They will also likely take on debt for investment purposes if they think there will be a larger payoff. Joel remembers former colleagues in late 2008 borrowing from their credit cards to invest in the market because of the ridiculous discounts (they were willing to borrow at a 20% interest rate or more for a year, all the while knowing that they would likely make at least 40% and they made more than 100%!).

Note: We are not advocating borrowing on your credit card to make investments if you don't have money available in the bank to do so. We are saying there may be some very special situations that may be advantageous, though risky. Please see our Ways to Invest, Chapter 6, for more information.

The benefits are: The Investor Type tends to earn a good ROI (Return on Investment). They are the ones who become financially free quickly. They believe that money works for them not the other way around. They also understand passive income and what it takes to become financially free, and how to calculate their financial freedom number.

The main reason to change from being an Investor is the same reason accumulators and protectionists should change. Often, The Investor Type will drive such a hard bargain, they will burn their bridges and have to hunt for new business partners and opportunities rather than develop relationships that are balanced and mutually beneficial. When you pursue a life of balance in which you include charitable giving and splurging on others, you will feel better about yourself and your relationship with your partner. Because you are allowing money to flow out into the world, it must come back to you. You will no longer just be investing your money. You will be sharing it with others for the greater good.

When an emergency comes up, investors tend to have plenty to cover those expenses. The Investor Types are in the best position of the seven money personality types. They can easily liquidate an investment, if necessary, to cover any emergency expenses.

Our Proposal: Our advice is similar to that for The Protectionist

Types and The Accumulator Types. The Investor Types are focused on each asset or item in their life being viewed as an asset or way to become financially free. Take some time to live in the moment and enjoy life as it is – without counting assets. Having more balance, especially if their partner is The Protectionist Type or The Type, is important. Consider what it would take to include other asset classes that would not be considered investments. Or setting up a charitable giving plan or a monthly splurge.

E stands for The Egotist Type

Their mindset is: as the name indicates, ego–driven. They believe they have the best financial plans. They tend to over–emphasize their own importance and skill when it comes to investments and money.

Their attitude: is one of confidence. They have an abundant mind-set. The Egotist Type is unconsciously overly optimistic with their in-vestments. They believe they know best regardless of any expertise available.

Their actions: include eager and confident investing. They believe no matter what investment they make, they will make money. It doesn't matter if it is a tip from a friend or bartender, or if they've done any research. The challenge with The Egotist Type is that they have not done sufficient research on their investments. Even so, their belief level is very high, but they are not mindful nor do they have a plan.

Because they have blinders on, they believe they will always make money in their investments. They do not consult with their partners and are often shocked when their partner doesn't agree with what they are doing.

The benefits are: The Egotist Types tend to invest their money and therefore, they do have a good chance of reaching their financial freedom goals. While they do have a savings account, they do not put all of their money there. They are excited about investing in new technologies and for the potential to make money in all new ideas.

When an emergency comes up, The Egotist Types tend to have

plenty to cover those expenses, assuming their overconfidence didn't cost them the whole investment, The Egotist Types should have money in their investments to liquidate so that they can cover emergency expenses.

The main reason to change from being The Egotist Type is the same reason The Investor Types should change: because when you pursue a life of balance in which you include charitable giving and splurging on others, you will feel better about yourself and your relationship with your partner. Like The Investor Types, The Egotist Types will no longer just be investing their money. They will be sharing it with others for the greater good.

When planning your change, one option would be to try to make a splurge once a week. Perhaps buy some flowers for your partner. Include your partner in the discussions.

Our proposal: We suggest that The Egotist Type consider your partner's point of view. Consider your partner's money personality type. Together research some options that work for the both of you. Then create a plan together.

Hot Hint! There is no right or wrong Money Personality Type. Our experiences make up who we are. And those experiences feed our Money Personality Type.

A Note About Giving:

No investor will ever talk about this, but it is probably the most powerful way to become financially free. Giving creates flow and good feeling. Both of which you want to perpetuate in your life. You reap what you sow!

Sir. John Templeton, considered by some to be the world's greatest investor, said that he didn't know anyone who had given 10 percent of what he earned to charities over a ten–year period who didn't massively grow his financial wealth.

Now, some of you may be thinking, "What? If I give my money

away, I will have less money. How does that work?" The reason is that money is energy—the more you give, the more you open yourself up to receive. The more you put that energy out into the world by giving and sharing with others, the more that energy must come back to you.

By giving as little as 10 percent, you are creating the belief that you are abundant and worthy and there is more than enough to go around.

When you open yourself up to giving, you open yourself up to receiving even more. The flow goes both ways. Giving can indeed change the world and we hope that this book inspires you to start.

So, how much do you spend on charitable giving versus just savings? Consider shifting the percentages more to the former and less on the latter. Keep a log of this on a monthly basis over the next six months. You will see small shifts that will ultimately lead to a complete change in your money personality type. Remember to take small baby steps. And remember to splurge as well (your partner will love it when you find something to splurge on for them)!

CHAPTER 1 EXERCISES

Exercise 1

Consider this scenario and answer which amount you would prefer.

You are offered a choice of $25,000 today or $1,000,000 in ten years. Which would you choose? Close the book and each write your answer down.

You would choose the million dollars correct? Well, you would if your goal was financial freedom.

Why?

Our thoughts are that some people prefer big rewards over smaller ones, but more people have an even stronger preference for money today over future rewards—even when the future rewards are 40 times the present compensation. You would have to earn a 45% return each year over the 10 years for the $25,000 to accumulate to $1,000,000 which has not been done by any professional money manager in history.

So, are you apt to "delay gratification" to the future to achieve your financial freedom or would you prefer immediate gratification? Some people have told us: "But if we had $25,000 today, we could pay off all our debt or we could buy a new house. Why wait ten years (to have a million dollars)?" Our answer is: Because to many people, $1,000,000 means financial freedom and even with the power of compound interest, $25,000 is very unlikely to accumulate to $1,000,000 in 10 years. So wait! Be patient! And make the right choice!

Discuss your choice with your partner! Make it fun, lively and interesting!

Exercise 2

Money Personality Types

1. Share your primary and secondary money personality types with your partner.

— Why do you resonate with these types?

2. Did the Assessment in the Appendix 1 differ from your self–assessment?

— Which money personality type would you prefer to ex-emplify?

3. Did you ever have a different money personality type?

— When and why do you think you changed?

4. Do you agree with your partner's self–assessment?

— Why or why not?

5. What do you think your partner's personality type is?

— Why do you think this?

6. How is your money mindset benefiting you?

— What changes can you make so that you can benefit?

Key Points From Chapter 1:

- Knowing your money personality type gives you the opportunity to know yourself better and adjust as needed.

- We believe your money personality type is fluid. It is likely that you have a primary and secondary money personality type. You may even have a tertiary money personality type.

- It is important to realize that you and your partner may have different primary personality types. Or that you and your partner may share the same primary type, and yet have differing secondary personality types. This can cause conflicts – and that is ok. Please see Chapter 11 – Recover and Resolve – to help you through them.

- We have a survey in Appendix 1 if you would like us to accurately assess which are your three most prevalent Money Personality Types since no one exhibits only one of them at all times.

- The acronym to remember is SUGA' PIE:
    - S stands for The Splurger Type
    - U for The Unconscious Type
    - G stands for The Greedy Type
    - A for The Accumulator Type
    - P stands for The Protectionist Type
    - I for The Investor Type
    - E stands for the Egotist Type

- See Appendix 2 for a Summary of Mindset, Attitude, Action Steps, Benefits and our Proposal to Change for each of the 7 Money Personality Types

CHAPTER 2:
FINANCIAL
BACKGROUNDS

The beginning of our parable:

"Did you know he didn't know anything about money??"

Natalie, my attorney, was nearly as exasperated as I was with my soon to be ex–husband. It was arbitration day. We were sitting in a middling conference room in a high rise. At least we were in downtown Seattle with a view of the Puget Sound. My ex–husband and his attorney were in another conference room down the hall. The arbitrator had just left our conference room to go back to speak with him.

"No." I sighed. "I didn't know until we were already married."

"What was your first clue?" She asked scoffing at me.

"Well, I had a little condo in Encino, California. It was just shy of 1,200 square feet. Though, the location was ideal, I had a mortgage on it as well as a second. The second was actually a personal loan from my dad. But believe me, I paid him before I ate. And there were times that I went without, just to pay him."

"So, if you couldn't afford it, why did you buy it?"

"Well, my dad was intent on teaching me about financing, credit scores, loans, and the benefits of property ownership. And, God bless him, I only struggled for about six months, and by the time I sold the property, the condo had actually doubled in value."

"I made a very tidy sum. On the other hand, my ex, had a home – in a far–away suburb of Seattle, two trucks, a boat, two snow mobiles, and an investment property in a tiny town in Eastern Washington. He made almost twice as much as I did, but couldn't make ends meet. This is because the interest rates he was paying on nearly everything were so high. He also paid a ton of maintenance on everything."

"What? Why?" She asked, intrigued.

"Well, he had terrible credit. He had some outstanding bills that were impacting his credit score. And they just remained on his credit report – unpaid, for years!"

I rolled my eyes. I continued, "When we first got together, I was in debt. But when I moved in to be with him, I sold my condo in California. And my financial issues disappeared. I was no longer in debt and even had additional money. On the other hand, while I did not know it before marrying him, I learned that he had bad credit. We tried to buy a property together but couldn't because his credit was so poor. So, we first had to clean up his credit."

"So that is why you're the primary on the joint house?" She asked, thinking she was piecing together the puzzle.

"Oh no! I am the primary owner because his credit was so poor and while we got most of it cleaned up before we bought the house, his credit score took time to recover. And while I had a condo, and he had a house, my home was comparatively in a much better location, so I made double what he made, even though his house was twice as big as mine. Plus, he spent much of his profits paying off his bad debts. On the other hand, being able to show a history of good investments, having cash on hand and having good credit made me the safer bet for the banks. So I became the primary. He had no background and an apparently poor understanding of finances. I guess I did not really know what his financial background was when I married him. Or how he developed his belief systems."

A relationship takes deliberate effort. It also is an effort to understand your own history and feelings behind your personality type. Further, sharing where your personality traits come from aid in the deeper understanding with your partner. It needs patience and curiosity. And most importantly, it needs intention. Therefore, it's important to be mindful. The first step to building that is to share the details of your life story; not just the chronology of your life, but the reasons for who you are and what makes you the special being you are. The background that led to your belief system and your money personality type.

Why is this necessary?

Well, knowing your own story means you know what you believe. And, more importantly, why you believe what you believe. Knowing these details helps us understand the culture we come from and the influences that shaped us. Getting to know your partner and what informs your partner's beliefs helps you in developing a better understanding and creating a deeper friendship with your partner.

Building a stronger relationship based on a deeper friendship helps grow a great connection. After all, the longest lasting relationships are based on that strong foundation of friendship and mutual respect, admiration and the understanding of each other's stories. We recommend knowing your partner at this deep love level for both money and life. This book will show you how to dive deeper into your financial relationship. If you are looking for a holistic approach to your relationship, check out Mollie's book: *Infinitely Loving: A Workbook to Support Couples in Creating a Life of Love Together*.

Money has a lot of emotion wrapped up into it. Money affects our lives in a great many ways. Our history with money – be it the first memory or any pivotal, especially early moment in life that had to do with money – is likely to affect us years beyond the actual moment.

Why?

Well, we need money to live. It is in our lives every day. And even if you think you are spiritually above the idea that "money makes the world go around," consider this: money is an exchange of *energy*.

Mollie recalls telling her beloved uncle once, that the pursuit of money wasn't everything. She said, "Money doesn't buy you happiness." And he responded with, "No. But it sure does buy you choices."

Socially, we are often told that the goal of life or of a relationship is to find happiness. But how do you define happiness? How does your partner define it?

Knowing that we come to this one word with different definitions helps us to deepen our understanding and bond with one another. After all, as in the example above, Mollie's definition of money was 'not happiness.' And her uncle's definition was 'choices.' So, who was right? Well, this is a trick question. Because they both are right. It is a matter of perspective. Having more choices may mean we need to make changes in our current ways of spending and saving.

How to Make Changes: In Exercise 2 below, we ask if you would like to see a change in the upcoming year. Changes can be approached in many ways.

Some of our favorite ways are:

- Small changes lead to big changes. When endeavoring to change any part of our lives, we should start small. We commit to one small change, incorporate that change into our lives, then make another small change. Pretty soon, the big change happens as if by magic. A great book to consider is *Little Bets* by Peter Sim. He makes the case for making small changes because "they allow us to discover new ideas, strategies, or plans through an emergent process, rather than trying to fully formulate them before we begin, and it facilitates adapting our approach as we go rather than continuing on a course that may lead to failure."

- A change in perspective. Sometimes just looking at the situation from a completely different viewpoint allows for a shift in your reality. For example, we can see the thorn bushes having some flowers. Or we can refocus and see those lovely roses first.

- Gratitude and understanding first. If you start by being thankful for what you have, and what is done for you, you set the Law of Attraction in motion and open yourself up to the same appreciation. Also, if you offer understanding before assumptions, the same love and grace is offered to you. This is a case of the Law of Attraction: what you offer the world is returned to you (Note: this is an internal process).

- Appreciate first. If you start by appreciating your partner, you set the Law of Attraction in motion to be appreciated. This is an external process. Therefore, it is important to share your appreciation with your partner. It is often the things that go unsaid that most need to be said. You can also recognize yourself and appreciate yourself. After all, our soul hears everything our mind says.

- Visualize. Andy Dooley, the creator of Vibration Activation™, says, "Feeling first, Manifestation second." Visualize what you want. Feel the feeling you want. And live in those feelings. You will surely manifest your desired change.

- Practice. Consistency is key. All change takes practice. In fact, to create a habit, you must consistently do your desired behavior for thirty days straight. F.M. Alexander, an Australian actor who developed the Alexander Technique, an educational process said to recognize and overcome reactive, habitual limitations in movement and thinking, said, "People don't decide their future. They decide their habits." Practice intention in your relationship. Every. Day. With love.

CHAPTER 2 EXERCISES

Exercise 1

- What is your first money memory? Take a moment to discuss with each other.

- What lasting impression did that first money memory make on you?

- Do you see an effect on your life today?

- What lesson did you glean from hearing your love's memory story?

Exercise 2

This first exercise is designed to help you understand the ways you and your partner view money, whether it is similar or different, and to begin the process of seeing some of the nuances you may not already know.

Hot Hint! This exercise may take some time. You may want to take a break after it. Whichever way you choose to proceed, remember to be patient with yourself and your love.

Consider the words in the table. Now, answer each question below for each word.

Words to consider:

Money	Retirement	Insurance
Cash	Travel/Vacation	Kid's College
Credit	Taxes	Bank Loans
Personal Loan	Earnings	Inheritance
Investments	Interest Rates	Emergency Expense

EXERCISES

Remember:

- Be open.

- Be curious – ask questions.

- Paint a detailed picture of your life story for your partner.

- Don't judge – your partner or yourself.

Questions to answer:

1. What do you associate with this word? Is it a positive or negative feeling?

2. Why do you think so?

3. Where does this association come from?

4. Have your thoughts or feelings changed in the last year? If so, how?

5. Do you want to see any changes in the upcoming year?

Did you gain a better understanding of your partner? You likely uncovered some things you did not previously know.

Let's dig deeper:

- Do you share your partner's definitions?

- Do you both believe the word being discussed is positive or negative?

- Do you need to do more digging to find common ground?

- How do you live with your differences?

- How well do we match up?

- What is our livable solution?

Hot Hint! The idea is to understand each other when you have different emotional responses to the various words in the table. You may wonder how a word such as "taxes" can illicit emotions. If for example, someone has back taxes, fear may be associated with that word. Or if someone feels they are paying too much in taxes, anger may be associated. Again, the idea is to fully understand each other's financial emotions. It helps to understand their motivations.

Exercise 3

Take a moment and ask each other the following:

- What was your biggest or most impactful money lesson as a child or young adult?

- What stands out to you most about it?

- Why is that the most important part of the story?

- How does that impact your life and finances today?

You may have noticed that we have included a lot of open—ended questions for your discussions. The idea is to get to know and love your partner for who they are...not for who you think they are or can become. The reality is, we all want to be loved for who we are...to get this, we need to have the love to give it.

Remember:

- You now know better where your partner is coming from, so be kind and receptive to your partner.

- Be open to influence. As you grow with your partner, your outlook on many topics can converge.

- Compare your answers and discuss what they mean to you and your partner.

Exercise 4

Share the answers with each other:

- How did your background experiences affect your finances?

- How did your background feed your money personality type?

- Did they help or hurt your finances?

- How do you unlearn those habits and become closer to your partner?

This book is here to show you how!

Before starting a conversation with your love, consider the following:

1. You may think you already know many things about your partner. However, saying, "I already know this about my partner" or any other alternative set of words implicitly presumes complete and accurate knowledge of our partner and immediately puts the brakes on the conversation. The fact is, we all continue to change. Keeping ourselves open, and open to each other is key. The goal of this book is to facilitate detailed and intimate conversations between the two of you.

2. Some of the topics may bring up fear and vulnerability. After all, we are talking about money – it is a sensitive topic for many. It is not always easy to be completely open with yourself, let alone with someone else. Know that the intention here is to create a safe space for you and your partner. We suggest these conversation starters as a way to open lines of communication for both of you.

Key Points From Chapter 2:

- Know each of your views and definitions of the various money terms. It is important to understand both your definitions and your partner's definitions, as well as the stories behind those definitions, because they form the foundation of your financial relationship.

- When you understand your partner's background, you have a joint place from which to grow. Now, you know how your partner developed their money personality type.

- You can make changes. Start small and be patient.

CHAPTER 3
EMOTIONS

We shift our perspective to our emotions, and back to our parable:

"And why did he have so much stuff?" Spitting the word "stuff" out like it was poison.

"Well, he liked to shop when he was sad. It helped him feel better. He also believed shopping was a way to celebrate...You know, we just had wildly different notions about money and finances. And sadly, we never connected and talked about it." I felt even sadder that I had never stopped to consider this.

"Which is why we are here!!" She looked at me pointedly.

"So, why was his credit so bad?" It almost looked like she was interested. Or maybe just bored. We had been there for hours with no real progress.

"Well, he was always so scared. He was afraid he owed too much and wouldn't be able to pay it. Even though he didn't actually owe that much. Apparently, collectors were constantly calling him. He was afraid to answer their calls. Or to even return any of the calls. Fear took over. And when he got really afraid, he would buy something to make himself feel better. He was the perfect mix of a person with both The Unconscious Type and The Splurger Type.

In the Financial Background Chapter – Chapter 2, we reviewed various financial words, the ways you both defined those words, and the significance of the definitions. Those definitions can evoke different emotions in both of you.

This chapter is designed to help you understand where your own emotions come from, which will then help you share the roots of who you are financially with your partner. In turn, it will help your partner get to know you better. And it will help you both to better navigate your lives with each other.

As Mike Dooley says, "Emotions are one of life's greatest gifts." They provide feedback on our progress in life, offering caution or encouragement as we go. When our emotions are pleasant, we are at peace and in alignment with our life. When they are unpleasant, we often feel unsettled and angst about our life.

So, where do our emotions come from? And what do they mean?

> Elisabeth Kübler–Ross, a Swiss–American psychiatrist and bestselling author of *Death and Dying* once said, "There are only two emotions: love and fear. All positive emotions come from love, all negative emotions from fear. From love flows happiness, contentment, peace, and joy. From fear comes anger, hate, anxiety and guilt. It's true that there are only two primary emotions, love and fear. But it's more accurate to say that there is only love or fear, for we cannot feel these two emotions together, at exactly the same time. They're opposites. If we're in fear, we are not in a place of love. When we're in a place of love, we cannot be in a place of fear."

When you think about finances, it can evoke many more nuanced emotions beyond love or fear. It will depend on the situations you are in; it can run the gamut from elation to anger to depression. But here is the secret: Emotions are a result of our perceptions, and our perceptions and perspectives actually arise from our beliefs. In other words, the beliefs discussed in the Financial Backgrounds chapter feed our emotions.

Your beliefs shape your perceptions and, therefore, create our emotions. How? Take the following table into consideration. See how your beliefs affect your perceptions and perspectives, and finally result in your emotions:

BELIEF	PERCEPTION/ PERSPECTIVE	TYPICAL EMOTION
People are loving and generous and want to be helpful.	I can trust my family and friends; I live in a safe and giving world.	Carefree, happy
People cannot be trusted; they will take advantage of you given the chance.	I cannot trust others. I could become a victim if I am not careful. Life is scary.	Scared, defensive
Money is no concern.	We have plenty to spare and share.	Comfortable, at ease
We don't have enough money.	We cannot afford to go on a vacation.	Insecure, afraid
I am a money magnet.	I will always be taken care of.	Abundance, prosperity
You have to work hard to be rich and successful.	Money is hard to come by.	Stress, envy
I am truly grateful for all the money I have.	I have money.	Safe, secure
Money will buy me happiness.	Money is the answer to everything.	Unworthiness, insecurity

Hot Hint! The middle column in the chart above is the foundation of a story you tell yourself. For example, if you are insecure about money and believe that money will buy you happiness, the *story* you tell yourself is that money is the answer to everything.

Understanding our own emotions helps us understand and shape ourselves. Understanding our partner's emotions helps us be more deliberate about creating a union filled with trust and love.

It is with the intent that we approach our money, our partners, and our lives that make a difference. If we save with the intention of growth, then as the Law of Attraction states, growth will happen. However, if we look to save with the intention of pinching our pennies, those are all we will be able to count.

For example, let's consider a trip to the grocery store. I have two options, one is to go from grocery store to grocery store to shop for the best savings on whatever I want to buy. With this tactic, I will likely save some money on the items on my list.

In this example, using the previous chart:

- My belief would be that I must be extraordinarily cost conscious.

- My perception/perspective would be that I do not have enough to pay for my groceries, or that my time is not worth that much.

- The emotions it evokes are insecurity and scarcity.

Consider this: going to several stores to get the best prices will actually cause me to lose time and money from the gas spent driving. And ultimately, the food I buy will be consumed with the intent of pinching pennies. It would represent scarcity lifestyle.

Conversely, if I go to one store for all of my groceries – even if it is a discount grocery store, the story I tell myself is that I value my time and that I have an abundant lifestyle. To take it a step further, you could splurge on one fancy jam to prove to yourself that you are abundant. And you could go one step further and donate a dinner to a shelter, proving to yourself that you have plenty to spare and share.

This grocery store example will demonstrate a story you are telling yourself about your beliefs regarding your abundance. Are you able to live in an abundant mindset with the fancy jam? Stories can end up ruling our present and affecting our future. Every time we give birth to a story based on our beliefs, perceptions and emotions, we forecast our future. Is the story you are telling yourself the future you desire?

If not, then understanding your emotions will help you understand how to adjust and shape the future you want. And understanding your partner's emotions will help you be more deliberate about creating a union filled with trust and love.

When your stories make you feel a negative emotion, they are fueled by limiting beliefs.

What is a limiting belief? It is a belief or a story that you are telling yourself that limits your possibilities. For example, if you think that you don't have the funds to shop at just one grocery store, you won't. As Henry Ford said, "Whether you think you can, or you think you can't, you are right."

As our emotions can be traced to our beliefs, limiting beliefs are almost always the cause of unpleasant emotions. For example, believing that you're unworthy, not smart enough, not good enough, or that the odds are against you, will eventually create emotions of sadness, anger and depression.

It is easy to identify negative emotions. However, it is not always as easy to identify the limiting belief behind that emotion.

Here is an example: My partner is always complaining about how late I work. Your limiting belief could be that your partner does not respect your work or wants you to quit. In reality, it may be that your partner just misses you. Or your limiting belief could be that you have to work hard to make good money. When in reality there may be other options out there for you.

**Please note – how to discuss these situations will be reviewed in Chapter 11 (Recover and Resolve). For now, we are simply discussing your beliefs.

Review, Reveal and Reverse – Your thoughts, words, and actions always reflect what's going on in your mind and what your beliefs really are. This technique involves Reviewing all that you think, say, and do. This will Reveal what your behavior is. When you catch yourself holding a negative thought or a limiting belief, you can reverse your thoughts to something more positive.

Practice Reviewing, Revealing, and Reversing one of your negative emotions. For example, using the limiting belief from above: My partner does not respect my work. Review that your partner loves you and wants to be with you. We like to find gratitude in our daily lives to see this. Then reframe the statement to yourself: My partner does not want me to work late because they want to spend time with me. The bonus of this reframing is that you will be coming at this from the point of love. The Law of Attraction tells us that love attracts more love.

Explain and Justify – This technique involves explaining and justifying all the reasons why you should have and deserve whatever it is that you want, and then acting the part. For example, write down as many of the reasons you can think of, explaining why your financial freedom is achievable and inevitable.

Remember, Emotions Sustain and Persevere

This is great news when we are in a good mood.

However, if we don't try to get a handle on our unpleasant and negative thoughts, not only can they bring us down in a moment with unpleasant emotions, but we can also begin to have unpleasant recurring experiences. Worse yet, our emotions can affect our partner, and vice versa. After all, you share your lives, you are connected and will feed off of each other's emotions. And those emotions spill into your finances. For example, if you are feeling fear about your job or the economy, you may stay at that very job that makes you unhappy out of fear. So, if you are in a negative head space, give yourself time to use one of the techniques to reframe and retell your story to yourself. Or better yet, ask your partner for help in the reframing. Include them in your headspace.

Remember that both the good and the–not–so–pleasant emotions are instructive. Emotions that are unpleasant can serve to open our hearts to deeper understanding and great life truths for ourselves, and for our partners. Should we want to change something, the good news is that joy and abundance are only a few thoughts away.

Since our beliefs and perceptions create our emotions, examining your beliefs and perceptions is where you can begin changing how you feel. Changing our perceptions is a little easier. Let's examine that first.

Changing your Perceptions

If we can see our challenges as providing gifts, we can change our perception of these challenges. Although our beliefs come first, followed by our thoughts, and then our emotions, we don't always have to start at the beginning with our beliefs to enact change. We can choose to find gratitude in the moment. That is not to take away from your current situation. It is simply to find the blessing in the situation. When we do so, and especially if we are able to hold onto that grateful emotion for 68 seconds, we start the change in our bodies and minds. According to Abraham–Hicks, holding a thought for 68 seconds will change your vibrational energy around the situation.

What is vibrational energy?

In chemistry, vibrational energy is the frequency at which atoms oscillate around a molecule. As all things are made up of atoms and molecules, everything creates energy. If you can change your perceptions to a more positive one, then you will change the energy that surrounds you, and therefore your situation.

We suggest giving it a try. All you have to gain is the Law of Attraction. And it only costs 68 seconds. Do not get discouraged if you do not manifest immediately. Please remember that the Universe is conspiring for your benefit. Keep visualizing, keep taking steps toward your goal, and you will succeed.

Hot Hint! To help further with changing your perceptions, try gratitude. Gratitude is one of the easiest emotions to access and initiate your change process. Look back at your life and uncover gifts you received from challenging circumstances or events that you have overcome (Gratitude is also Rule #6 in Joel's Bestseller, *The 9 Money Rules Millionaires Use: Only The Unconventional Ones*).

Usually we perceive challenges as negative, but every challenge we encounter brings us gifts. Can you find gratitude in the gift of the challenge? After all, these gifts make us better than who we were before the challenge arose. When examining a prior challenge that we have already dealt with, this exercise is easy.

For example:

My partner lost their job. The silver lining or hidden gift is finding a new job that can be better and more rewarding. Or realizing that we get to spend more time together, and my partner has time to figure out what they really want. Or we get more time to re–evaluate our lives and we get an opportunity to redesign our lives into what we really want.

The Big Picture – Understanding Your Emotions

Experiencing some emotional pain in your life is unavoidable. However, pain can give birth to new insights. Allowing your partner to hear your pain is an important part of building a life together. As you face your pain together, you grow together.

Note: We are not suggesting that a loss of any sort is going to be easy. We understand that there will be some negative emotions and impact around it. There will be concerns. However, we *are* suggesting a technique to arrest the negative spiral. Recalling that emotions perpetuate and persevere, we want you to find your way to positive emotions. And recall what Abraham—Hicks tells us about positive thoughts.

Dealing with Emotions

Sometimes we have a bad day. Or sometimes, we are just cranky. Other times, we have a misunderstanding with each other. Either way, unpleasant emotions come up. There are ways to deal with these emotions. The first thing to do is understand all of our emotions. In Mollie's book, *Infinitely Loving: A Workbook to Support Couples in Creating a Life of Love Together*, you will find a more extensive list of emotions and a deep dive exercise on how to handle them.

Building Connections. Love attracts more love.

You show love in big and small ways. Build on the love you already share by deepening your friendship. It is the building block of your relationship. It heightens your love and attachment for one another just like the bouquet of flowers, the random sticky note of love, and words of appreciation.

Practice

Take a moment this week to write and share what you love and appreciate about your partner. Just write what you admire — be it within your relationships, or outside.

Please remember to share this note with your partner.

Consider:

- How does writing this note make you feel?

- How did it feel to receive this note?

- Are these loving feelings ones that you would like to keep going?

Write more love notes and notes of appreciation for your partner. As Mollie teaches in her workbook, *Infinitely Loving: A Workbook to Support Couples in Creating a Life of Love Together*, connecting with others, showing love and wooing your partner is a life–long process.

Please remember, it is those things that most often need to be said that sadly often go unsaid. Share your loving emotions with your partner.

CHAPTER 3 EXERCISES

Exercise 1

Take a moment to recall the last financial decision you made. Now, discuss each of your emotions, perceptions and beliefs with each other.

- Did you think of the same decision?
  - If not, discuss both situations.
  - Were they individual decisions? Or a joint decision?
  - Should it have been one or the other?

- Name three emotions that came from that decision you just thought of separately.

- What were your perceptions behind each of the emotions?

- What belief system did each emotion reveal?

- What did you learn about your partner and the handling of the decision?

As you review this exercise, you will notice that you just laid the foundation of a story. So, what are the stories behind each of your emotions? Take a moment to share with each other. Did you have a different story than your partner? If so, take a moment to discuss.

Exercise 2

Use each one of these questions as a full conversation starter.

- What does financial freedom mean to you?

- Why is it achievable and inevitable?

- Why do we want financial freedom?

- Why are we working on getting to a deeper level of understanding ourselves?

Our answer to the last question is: To find happiness, and to build deeper connections with our partner. The more we understand and love, the more we are understood and loved. It is the Law of Attraction.

Exercise 3

Consider a financial decision that made you feel a negative emotion. What story are you telling yourself based on that emotion? Please refer to the chart on page 38 to help with identifying your story.

Do you want a different story? If so, what story would you prefer?

- Tell each other your original story, then share your preferred story – even if it is acknowledging that you are telling yourself the story you want to hear.

- Use one of the techniques listed above – either "Review, Reveal, and Reverse" or "Explain and Justify" to help tell your new story.

- Do you want to be part of the story your partner is telling? If not, discuss what you would prefer.

Exercise 4

What were your greatest financial challenges and what was the silver lining or hidden gift you found?

Each of you, take a moment to share with each other one of your past greatest challenges.

- Tell the story behind that challenge.

- What was your silver lining or hidden gift from that challenge?

Share and discuss with your partner.

And what about your challenges today?

What if you could change how you perceive your greatest challenge in the here and now? If you could realize right now that it is making you better, wouldn't this completely change how you feel about it?

Armed with the new understanding that your feelings and emotions feed your story, what would be your new story?

- Tell the story behind that challenge.

- What can your hidden gift from that challenge be?

Share and discuss with your partner.

Exercise 5

In this exercise, we will review some words for you to consider. To help you better understand each other, consider each word. Discuss each question with each other.

Words to consider:

Happiness, Peace, Gratitude, Fear, Anger, Guilt

Questions to discuss:

- What causes you to feel that emotion?

- What experiences create that emotion?

- <u>For: Happiness, Peace and Gratitude</u>: How do you want to celebrate that emotion?

- How can you express your feelings to your partner?

- What could your partner do to help celebrate that emotion?

- <u>For: Fear, Anger, Guilt</u>: How do you want to recover from that emotion?

- How can you express your feelings to your partner?

- What could your partner do to help when you are feeling that emotion?

Exercise 6

What does your partner do that inspires the emotions of love and appreciation? Be specific.

List 5 qualities you cherish about your partner and give specific examples of when they exhibited each quality.

Share with your partner.

Key Points from Chapter 3

- Discuss each of your emotions, perceptions and beliefs with each other.

- A limiting belief is a belief or a story that you are telling yourself that limits your possibilities.

- We suggest using two techniques to change your own limiting beliefs: Review, Reveal, and Reverse & Explain and Justify.

- Emotions sustain and persevere.

- If you can see your challenges as providing gifts, you can change your perception of these challenges.

- Gratitude is one of the easiest emotions to access and initiate your change process.

- Love attracts more love. You show love in big and small ways. Build on the love you already share by deepening your friendship.

CHAPTER 4:
EMOTIONAL SCENARIOS

In this section, we provide you with three scenarios. For each scenario, we will ask a few questions for you to consider. These questions are designed to help facilitate a conversation between the two of you.

We have specifically not shared our answers and opinions. Everyone will read these situations differently and will have different perspectives. In our real lives, we will experience things differently as well. The idea is to pause, reflect on what it means to you, share that with your partner, and understand what it means to them. In this way, you will be able to get to know each other even better and know how you can navigate your finances together.

Scenario 1:

"Where did those come from?" She fumed.

"Oh I saw them in Macy's yesterday. They are gorgeous! I mean, not as gorgeous as you, but I just had to have them!" He said full of glee.

"Ok. How much?" She demanded. She had to know.

"They were only $1,500. Isn't that great. Over 50% off what they normally go for," he exclaimed again full of joy.

"Are you kidding me? For cufflinks?!? You don't wear cufflinks. You don't even have a shirt that needs cufflinks! And, seriously, you know how much debt we have already! How are we going to pay for this?" She asked, exasperated.

"What? Really! I thought you would be happy with the amazing deal I got," he said surprised. "Plus, this is for your parents' party!"

"Come On! We didn't discuss this expense. When are you going to understand our money situation?"

1. Can you name three emotions each person in this scenario may have felt?

2. Does this bring up any emotions for you?

3. Was there open communication?

4. What would you tell each party in this scenario?

5. What could have been done differently?

Scenario 2:

"How much did we make?" She asked hopefully.

"Well, that's a great question," her partner responded with a hint of trepidation.

"What's going on?" She was starting to get that feeling of dread.

"Well, it was a great idea. I know you had gotten the intuitive hit on that stock and your intuition is quite strong. And even though we talked about it, I decided we should paper trade this one. You know, just pretend that we were buying it. So, I put $10,000 in the fake account."

"What!? Why?" The feeling of dread turned into incredulity.

"Well, to be honest with you," he started slowly. "Here is the thing hun: The stock market has been so volatile" (in 2020) that I was thinking: what if the market collapses like it did in March? Everything went down that month even the best companies. And some collapsed 40%...in just 4 weeks! So, why risk it?" He finished.

Wait. So, are you telling me, because you were scared, we missed out on over $2,000 in gains in just a couple of days! What!?"

1. Can you name three emotions each person in this scenario may have felt?

2. Does this bring up any emotions for you?

3. Was there open communication?

4. What would you tell each party in this scenario?

5. What could have been done differently?

Scenario 3

"I hate this feeling. I know it's feeling first manifestation second, but I am truly wallowing in despair and anxiety!" He explained to me.

"Why" I asked? "What changed? You were doing so well last month!" I responded.

"Well, my wife shared a spreadsheet with me. I swear, she is such a drama queen!"

"Roll it back, start from the beginning with me. And while you are at it, do you think there is truth in what she is saying?"

"Well, sure, I tend to bury my head in the sand when it comes to budgeting and finances and well, she may be good at it. And sure, I let her do it all...she loves it anyway. She showed me the spreadsheet documenting that we had accumulated $17,000 of credit card debt. I really thought we were in a different place financially. I had started saving on my own, and I had been making huge progress in my retirement fund. Now, I have to hand half of it over to our joint account. I am back to being so afraid!"

"What are you most afraid of?" I inquired.

"Well, obviously, retirement...not being able to retire. You know I'm 61 and I really want to stop working in 4 years. Is that even possible? Both my children are getting married next year. And I want to do what is right, especially for my daughter, but I don't think my wife wants to fund anything. That means I'm going to have to limit retirement savings again for the next year to put aside money for the weddings."

"Anyway, today's news of being in debt really overwhelmed me. I can't handle it. Will I ever be able to retire? I am really worried and so depressed today. Can you help?"

1. Can you name three emotions each person in this scenario may have felt?

2. Does this bring up any emotions for you?

3. Was there open communication?

4. What would you tell each party in this scenario?

5. What could have been done differently?

CHAPTER 5:
WAYS TO SAVE

Is Being a Saver good or bad?

Recall our couple getting divorced, There was one big spender with a money personality of The Splurger Type, and one who kept the budget, with a money personality of The Accumulator Type.

The Splurger Types enjoy spending and accumulating material things. Typically, they tend to be collectors. We saw this with the husband's collection of a second house, a boat, and snow mobiles. Conversely, like the wife in the story, The Saver Types are generally risk–averse, meaning they are not interested in risking their money. They are all about safety and security. We saw this with her responsible behavior to bad credit and spending.

The Accumulator Types do their best to include their partner in all their decisions around money and make their partner feel safe and secure about their financial future.

Recall from Chapter 1: The Accumulator Type can lean towards a scarcity mentality. They tend to prioritize savings over living expenses. For example, they may not replace a worn out couch for many years in hopes of saving more money. The focus is making sure they never have to worry about money. This is ironic though, because that creates a feeling of lack. It sets off a vibrational frequency that, given the Law of Attraction, attracts even more lack. That said, it is good to plan for the future, but if you are always worried (we define that as "negative future planning") then you will keep your money in saving and checking accounts instead of having your money work for you (like the investors do).

Again, as the Law of Attraction tells us, instead of always worrying about the bad weather, think about what you do want to happen: the bright sunny, cloudless days. And more of those happy days will come your way.

Recall your work in Chapter 1: You may have previously, or may even still, consider yourself The Splurger Type or The Accumulator Type. Revisit what those words mean to you. And remember, you are a multi–dimensional being. So, if you want to feel more secure and splurge every now and again, you can! And if you want to learn to save more, you can! And we are here to help you.

Is being The Splurger Type or The Accumulator Type good or bad? Being only one or the other is not good. Life is rarely black and white. If you are only accumulating, or saving your money, you are not allowing the flow to happen. You should give some money away, spend some on others or invest it. That way, you are putting that money out into the world.

Hot Hint! Money, like air, needs to flow. And for you to breathe in air, you must also breathe out air. Similarly, abundance, in this case, money, won't flow back to you in multiples of what you put out there, unless you actually put *something* out there.

Saving, Spending, and Investing, Oh my!

Let's discuss coffee and other daily decisions you make every day. Does that coffee really make a difference? As a couple, you must decide whether to get that Grande Mocha Caffe for about $4.50 daily or not.

Well, consider the alternative. Again, we are not against the monthly feel–good splurge. However, buying that Grande Mocha Caffe daily every day for a year means over $1,700 could have been accumulated in an investment. Imagine you could do this for 10 years, then that Caffe would accumulate to almost $25,000!! And if you invested that $25,000, it would grow dramatically year over year.

What is Saving?

Mollie: What does savings mean to you?

Joel: To me, savings means freedom.

Mollie: Tell me more!

Hot Hint! *Ask questions to learn about your partner! Even if you think you already know the answer – ask for more details. Be nosey!*

Joel: When I have enough money saved, I can do what I want for as much time as I want. To me, that really is financial freedom. That's what savings and investing is: you're doing what you love, with whom you love, for as much time as you love.

And what do you *want* to do?

Let's talk more specifically about savings. What types of accounts can you save money in?

First of all, most of us still have money in a bank: even if it is just in a checking account.

When is the last time you balanced your checkbook?

Does anyone do that anymore?

How much are you spending on various items? This is a great starting point to play the Budget Game (see Where is Your Cash Going? – Chapter 15).

Did your deposits get credited?

Do the withdrawals look right?

Can you quickly add up the deposits and withdrawals to check that the starting balance plus the deposits less the withdrawals equals the ending balance?

That is called balancing your checkbook!

It is important to note that the following discussion on checking accounts, certificates of deposit (CDs), Treasury bills, notes, and bonds, is based on the interest rate environment in 2021. In future years, interest rates may be substantially higher which may imply that using these savings vehicles might actually be prudent—assuming inflation stays relatively sanguine. If you have questions about these accounts, feel free to reach out to Joel for your 30–minute free prosperity coaching session:
https://app.acuityscheduling.com/schedule.php?owner=16345620

How much interest is being credited to your checking account?

In 2021, most banks were crediting less than 0.1% to your checking account. There were a few online banks crediting 1%. You can get the average rate from bankrate.com.

Should you go for the highest rate out there to earn 1% more? Our recommendation is "No!" There are likely to be many restrictions on your cash to get the higher rate.

One restriction is likely to be that you must keep a certain amount of cash in the account which will be relatively high. Most checking accounts in 2021 have a very low or no minimum balance. The checking accounts paying 1% interest are likely to require a much higher minimum balance.

A second restriction may be that you can't set up overdraft protection so that if you don't have funds to pay a bill, you can't automatically borrow and the bank will charge you a significant fee—as high as $50.

The third restriction is likely to be access to your money. If you are not at one of the local community or national banks, you are likely to have to pay a fee to get money out of an ATM.

If you say, "Well, I don't need cash anymore." Then go for it, but make sure that if you are using credit cards, you pay them off monthly!

Bank savings accounts usually pay a bit more. Though, in 2021, the highest rates were still only about 1%.

Certificates of Deposit (CDs) are still around, but rarely used and we don't recommend them.

A CD pays a fixed interest rate if you keep your money in it for the whole specified term. These can be as short as three months and, as long as, five years. The highest rate, at the time of publishing, the long–term five–year CDs is 2.3%.

Why lock up your money for five years for an extra 1%? Our opinion is that interest rates are likely to be much higher in 2024 than 2021. So, don't do it. By putting your money into a CD for more than a year, you are effectively making an interest rate bet: that interest rates will be no higher than they are now. Not the most rational bet in 2021.

Also, if you have to take the money out before the five years are up, you will be charged with an early withdrawal fee.

One step up from bank CDs are money market funds. These funds—also known as money funds—are not insured by the banks. They tend to pay a little higher interest rate than bank CDs though, in early 2021, the money market fund interest rates were also about 1–1.25%. The benefit of the money market fund, though, is you have access to your money whenever you want it. There is no term or penalty for taking your money out early like there is for a bank CD. Though, there are often a limited amount of times per month that you can make withdrawals.

Treasury bills are U.S. government–backed debt obligations that you invest in for less than one year. Treasury bills are sold in denominations of $1,000. These investments are considered low risk, but there is no guarantee despite being "backed by the U.S. government."

In mid–2020, the one–year Treasury bill was crediting less than 0.2% or 20 bps (bps is a financial term used by traders and investors indicating basis points. Basis Points are one 100th of one percent.). A five–year Treasury note was crediting less than 0.5% or 50 bps. And a ten–year Treasury bond was crediting less than 0.75% or 75 bps.

We would not recommend investing in bonds with the extremely low interest rates present in 2021. The biggest risk is that interest rates go up and you miss out on a much higher interest rate environment by investing in five–year or ten–year Treasuries (and, of course, if you decide to buy different bonds in a higher interest rate environment by selling your Treasuries, their value would have gone down).

Let's discuss inflation. The biggest risk to investing in these securities—CDs or Treasury bills or notes or bonds—that "appear" to be very safe is inflation. Though the consumer price index for inflation in 2020 was much less than 1% and has been less than 2% for the last few years, inflation does impact your cost of living and the "official" index may not be the best indicator of how much your personal cost of living has increased lately. The index measures a mix of various items that may not be representative for you and your partner personally. If you spend a high percentage of your income on healthcare and housing costs, then inflation was over 5%.

Now the importance of inflation is how your returns compare to your cost of living, especially if it was almost all housing and healthcare. Then, in approximately 15 years, you would need twice as much money to pay for the same level of housing and healthcare.

For example: Let's say you have a CD for $10,000 and it earns as high as 2%. In 2021, it will have to be a minimum deposit time of 1 year. In that one year, inflation will go up by 5%.

$10,000 * 2% = $10,200

Inflation = $500

Therefore, you actually lost $300.

As you can see, a CD is actually not risk free.

How have your investments performed?

Well, if you are relying on Treasury bonds earning 0.75% (75 basis points), you've definitely lost a significant amount of money. Similarly, your 5–year CD (assuming it stayed at the same rate as 2020) earned you a 7% return over 15 years. But everything cost 100% more!

As you can see, there are many ways to save – all of which include reviewing your spending choices. Of course, we advocate spending as it allows for flow. We *also* advocate reviewing your savings and your investments plans together. The next chapter will talk about ways to invest. Choose what works for the both of you.

Some key questions we've been asked about spending are:

I am in the market for a new car. Should I buy a new car or a used car?

First, a car is *not* an investment. A car is an asset that depreciates over time. We do not recommend buying a new one because it depreciates 20% or more as soon as you drive it off the lot. And most cars have lost close to 50% of their value in five years! Also, its value is going down since you are using it to drive for pleasure or to work.

Our strong preference is to buy a used car—maybe 2 years old—or lease—depending on the financing rate you can get on the lease and the expected amount of time you own the car or the miles you plan to drive the car. As a bonus, you can have the feeling of abundance as you can afford a more luxurious version with upgraded features of your chosen car because you have chosen a slightly older model.

If you are considering leasing, and you expect to drive more than 12,000 miles per year, then we suggest that you buy the used car. Most automobile dealerships charge an extra fee if you go beyond your allocated miles making the lease a poor choice. There are high mileage leases which effectively charge more by increasing the monthly lease payment, another option we do not suggest.

Also, consider the rate of the loan, if you can't pay for the used car in cash. In 2021, the interest rate on used car loans ranged from 4–5% depending on if you were borrowing for 3–5 years.

How much should I spend on my wedding and all the accoutrements, like the dress? Should the wedding be intimate or lavish? A local wedding or a destination wedding?

Whether you are discussing your own upcoming wedding, or a planning a wedding for your children, this is a very important discussion to have. We understand that for many men and women this is a very personal discussion. It brings up feelings from childhood and perhaps some issues that relate to money as well: fear, greed, and "keeping up with the Joneses!"

We have a discussion just for you below. Take a break and have that discussion now on this critical topic. Or, if you have children, consider if and/or how much you want to save for their wedding. As you discuss your feelings about weddings, remember your work in the Financial Backgrounds chapter – Chapter 2.

Here are our points of view on the subject:

Come up with an overall budget first.

Consider how much of your savings (or investments) you feel comfortable spending on the wedding in total. The budget will include all the items including the honeymoon costs. We have heard of middle–class couples spending more than $100,000! And this does *not* include the honeymoon! Imagine that money invested over the next ten or twenty years!

So, come up with your budget first. This will inform all future discussions.

According to Weddingstats.org, here are the average costs of the items needed for a wedding in 2020. Remember, this is the average and as discussed above, each couple should decide where they would like to spend more (or less) on a particular item:

1. Venue – $16,107

2. Photographer – $2,783

3. Reception band/music – $4,156

4. Florist – $2,534

5. Videographer – $1,995

6. Wedding dress – $1,564 (not including the corset, petticoat, veil nor shoes)

7. Groom's attire – $280

8. Wedding cake – $582

9. Ceremony site – $2,197

10. Ceremony musicians – $755

11. Invitations – $462

12. Transportation – $859

13. Favors – $268

14. Rehearsal dinner – $1,378

15. Engagement ring – $6,163

16. Officiant – $278

17. Catering (price per person) – $71

18. Wedding day hair care – $119

19. Wedding day make–up – $100

If you add these items up, you get about $43,000. We have heard that an average wedding dress alone, though, could be as much as $10,000 (not the $1,564 shown above, which would make the total wedding cost over $50,000).

Also, many people we know have asked about having a destination wedding. We believe this is really a personal preference.

It can be really fun for the couple especially if this is used as a jumping off point for their honeymoon nearby. A destination wedding could add a considerable expense, especially if the couple is paying for the attendees to get there. Conversely, it can also considerably cut down on the expenses if the couple is choosing to let the destination be on "display" and have the attendees pay for their own travel and accommodations.

How often should we vacation? What kind of vacations do we take? Should we budget each one or go first class?

Again, our recommendation is to have a discussion. What do vacations mean to each of you? What kinds of vacations do each of you like? Are these financial freedom trips or annual or quarterly trips?

We both love traveling and, thankfully, we have found partners who do too.

Joel likes to take vacations quarterly. His ideal is to travel internationally (outside the U.S.) at least once a year and have vacations that are active, adventurous, as well as historical city tours. His children, like the island and beach trips, which he also enjoys once a year.

Mollie and her husband like to *plan* at least one international trip annually. But they find themselves on at least two a year. She also peppers in several trips to see Broadway shows in New York, or to visit friends and relatives on the west coast throughout the year.

We recommend setting a budget for annual travel and sticking to it. Especially, post–2021, we believe there will be many ways to achieve cost–effective travel and still have what was considered in the past, a "high–end" vacation. When you choose your travel plans, we recommend checking out news events and weather patterns to pick your destinations. For example, 2022/2023 may prove to be a great time to go on a cruise.

Do you have a Will or a Trust?

It is a good idea to have your final wishes listed out. A Will or Trust requires a list of assets and liabilities (see Where is Your Cash Going, Chapter 15 for definitions and the types of each). Plus, here you can list your final wishes. If you haven't discussed this before, it's time to close the book and do it NOW!

Now, who oversees the finances or do both of you participate?

If you have separate checking or savings accounts, what percentage of your monthly income will go into the joint account? Consider putting a set percentage of each paycheck into your own account and then put the rest into the joint account. This allows for the freedom to still surprise your partner if you decide to splurge on them.

How can you ensure there are no overdrafts if you both are drawing from the account for a big purchase or a credit card bill?

Have the discussion!

And remember, whenever discussing money, you both should exercise caution during the conversation. Money questions can unintentionally trigger our emotions. In Mollie's book, *Infinitely Loving: A Workbook to Support Couples in Creating a Life of Love Together*, she goes into detail on how to handle Differences and Conflict Resolution. It is worth noting that you should get the story behind each other's feelings. And ask how to help each other make things better. We will also review the financial version of this in Chapters 10 and 11, Conflict, and Recover and Resolve, respectively.

Chapter 5 Exercises – Do these exercises if a wedding is in your future.

Exercise 1

Consider the following words:

- Wedding
- Guests
- Dress
- Venue
- Honeymoon
- Food
- Flowers
- Photographer
- Guest lists

And consider the following questions for each of the words above:

- How do you feel when you hear this word?
- Where does that feeling come from?
- Is there a dream behind this word? If so, what is it?
- Is this an emotional trigger? If so, what is triggered?
- Do you want to change this emotion?

Exercise 2

Take a moment to discuss:

What type of wedding do you want?

Do you want a lavish wedding? Or an intimate affair?

Do you want it local? Or destination?

What does it mean to you?

Where do those feelings come from?

Can you get those feelings from something else?

Key Points from Chapter 5:

- Life is rarely black and white. If you are only accumulating, or only saving your money, you are not allowing for the flow to happen. You should give some away, spend some on others and/or invest it. That way, you are putting that money out into the world. Money, like air, needs to flow. Conversely, if you are only spending, you are not allowing for inflow.

- Consider how much of your savings (or investments) you feel comfortable spending on large purchases such as a wedding. The budget will include all the items including the honeymoon costs.

- Should you go for the highest rate out there to earn 1% more? Our recommendation is "No!" There are likely to be many restrictions on your cash to get the higher rate.

- The biggest risk to investing in these securities — CDs or Treasury bills or notes or bonds — that "appear" to be very safe is inflation.

CHAPTER 6:
WAYS TO INVEST

Retirement savings vehicles

What are they? Where do I begin?

Annuities are examples of retirement savings vehicles. You put money into these accounts after–tax (we highly recommend not investing in annuities within your Individual Retirement Accounts, see below). Annuities can be fixed or variable. A fixed annuity is one in which you put in a lump sum or invest over time and the insurance company credits you an interest rate that is fixed based on their ability to invest in bonds and other investments.

In 2021, a five–year fixed annuity was crediting between 2.5–3%. Annuities have penalty fees in case you want your money before the end of the term—just like a CD.

You can also invest in a variable annuity which has a minimum crediting rate—currently less than 1%. This annuity invests in various types of mutual fund options and there is no guarantee that you will get that return.

All annuities have surrender charges if you want your money before the term is up. They are usually consistent with the term of the annuity. If you buy a 7–year annuity, then the surrender charge starts at 7% and declines 1% a year until the last year when it is 0%. If you buy a 5–year annuity, then the surrender charge starts at 5% and declines 1% a year until the last year when it is 0%.

401(k) Plans

Many employers offer a 401(k) plan to employees as part of their benefits package. The plan provides a tax deduction for both the employer and the employee when the employee puts money into their 401(k) account. While the main idea is that you put money into the plan pre–tax, it helps to understand how these contributions work.

Normally, when you earn money as an employee, you have income taxes withheld on the money you earn. A traditional 401(k) plan allows you to avoid paying income taxes in the current year on the amount of money you put into the plan. The amount you put in is not taxed, so you 'defer' your tax payment until later.

The money grows tax deferred inside the traditional 401k plan. Tax deferred means that while the investments earn investment income, you do not pay tax on the investment gains each year. Instead, in retirement, you pay tax only on the amounts you withdraw at that time and you are likely to be in a lower tax bracket in retirement and, therefore, likely to be taxed less as well. You'll pay a 10 percent penalty tax and income taxes if you withdraw funds too early (before age 55 or 59½, depending on your retirement age).

Withdrawing funds early usually happens during an emergency. However, we do urge you to consider your options. Is it a true emergency? Is it better or worse to get a different type of loan? For example, if you absolutely need the funds, then it may be better to pay the fees associated than to get a cash advance from your credit card if that interest rate is upwards of 18%. In any case, please weigh your options carefully.

In 2021, there were two types of 401ks. The traditional ones which we just described and the Roth 401k. A Roth works a little differently in that they don't offer the up–front tax break on your contributions. In a Roth 401k, you pay tax on your income as you normally would and then make after–tax contributions. Once your money is in this 401k fund, you don't ever have to pay taxes on it again.

What is so awesome about the 401k is that most companies will match how much you invest up to a certain amount. We look at that as free money! Look what you just manifested!!

For most companies, the match is 3%. So, we recommend putting at least the minimum amount of what is matched into the 401k. Effectively you start out with a 100% return on your money, assuming you become vested. Vesting is an amount of time a company sets for the minimum term of your employment. Once that term is up, you get the match amount in your 401(k).

Suppose you are earnings $100,000 and you put in 3% or $3,000 a year. Even if the fund you chose (we'll get to that in a second!) earns a 0% return, you will have $6,000 in your 401k at the end of the year! Now suppose in year 2, you earn a 10% return and you still put only the 3% minimum to get the 100% match from your company. At the end of year 2, you have put in $6,000.

How much do you have in your account? Well, the $6,000 of monies at the end of year 1 earned $600 and the $6,000 you put it in year 2 earned $300 (since it was invested on average a half a year) and you have $12,900 at the end of year two and you only invested $6,000 of your own money (a return of more than 140% annually!). That is why it really makes sense to invest in your 401k.

Now remember, we don't include these monies in your financial freedom amount because you can't get access to that money (without penalties or a high–interest loan) until at least 59½. And the only amounts that are included towards your passive income number are amounts that you are earning money on today!

What funds should you invest in? We recommend using a market index fund like the S&P 500 (these are the 500 largest companies in the stock market) or a Russell 2000 (this is mostly smaller companies) index. These funds have the lowest fees and eliminate the risk of choosing a fund that significantly underperforms the market.

Avoid all those funds that include bonds which have various names like "balance mutual funds" or "hybrid funds" or "target date funds," which were so popular in 2021. Remember Treasury bonds were earning approximately 1% and bonds issued by corporations were only generating a 2–4% return in 2021.

A Roth IRA (Individual Retirement Account) is a special retirement account that you fund with post–tax income (you can't deduct your contributions on your income taxes). Once you have done this, all future withdrawals that follow Roth IRA regulations are tax–free. There is no up–front tax deduction for Roth IRA contributions as there is with a traditional IRA; on the other hand, Roth distributions are tax–free. And because every penny you stash in a Roth IRA is your money, you can tap your contributions (but not your earnings on those contributions) at any time, tax–free and penalty–free.

Are there other ways to save and invest?

Absolutely. Many people we know use life insurance and annuities as savings vehicles. Let's start with life insurance. There are two types of life insurance: term insurance and insurance with a cash value. Term insurance is exactly what it sounds like. You have the insurance for a specific period of time or term. It can be 10 years or 20 years or more. Term insurance is pure insurance. You pay your monthly or annual premium and if you die before the period of time is up, your heirs or beneficiaries get the amount of the policy, also known as the face amount. There is no savings element here.

There are two types of term insurance. You can buy a "level premium" policy which is exactly what it says. You pay the same premium for the term: 10 years or 20 years. An annual renewable term policy has a premium that goes up each year over the term of the policy. Importantly, neither of these policies require a medical exam after you are approved for coverage.

The other type of insurance is cash value life insurance. This type of policy comes in many names: whole life insurance, universal life, variable universal life, or survivorship whole life. These are the policies that you can use to save money. But should you?

There are a number of considerations:

1. What is the implicit return on the policy, or what can I expect to earn? With whole life or universal life policies, you get an "illustration" of what you can expect to earn. There is no guarantee you will earn this. It will depend on how well, the investment department of the insurer you choose, invests your funds. With a "variable" policy, you get to choose the un-

derlying mutual funds that the policy invests your money in. If you choose well, you can earn a higher return than the "fixed" return that the company generates for you. If you choose poorly, you might earn a much lower return. You should take into consideration yours and your partner's money personality type as well as both of your risk tolerance.

2. What is the surrender charge or penalty you incur when you want to get access to your money? This is usually very high in the early years of the policy and much lower after, say, 10 years.

3. Are you already putting the maximum into other retirement savings plans like your 401k plan at work? If so, cash value life insurance could be a consideration, though again, what is the return that the insurance company can generate? In 2021, the expected cash value return for fixed policies is approximately 4–5%.

Now why is cash value life insurance "pitched" on those late–night infomercials or on your favorite social media site as a great "forced–savings" plan? Because part of your premium is going to the cash–value build–up of the policy and you can surrender the policy and get that cash (less the penalties). In the past there have been life insurance companies that did not disclose that it was a life insurance policy – not just a savings plan. Please be sure you are aware of what you are signing up for.

It is important to consider what your rate of return is on your money, though. Suppose you put $1,000 a year into your $100,000 cash value policy. After 10 years, you have put in $10,000. And at the end of the 10 years, you have $13,000 of cash value.

Sounds great right?

If you want that money, your fee is 4% and you can have access to $12,350 if you surrender the policy.

In reality, the return on your $10,000 is only about 5% per year.

Could you do better in other investing plans like a 401k? That is highly likely.

You can also borrow against the policy. In this case, you can get access to the cash value, but you have to pay interest on the borrowings. In 2021, the typical rate was 8%. So, if you wanted to get access to $30,000, you would have to pay $2,400 a year, as long as the $30,000 is outstanding. This rate of interest is higher than most personal loans and much, much higher than a home equity loan in 2021. And it's your money!

Some common questions about life insurance:

I've heard that you are supposed to buy life insurance when you are young since it costs less. Is it true?

It is true that your annual premium is lower if you purchase life insurance at 25 instead of 55 because the probability of you dying is higher at 55. But insurance salespeople don't explain that you will have been paying the premiums for 40 years instead of 10 if you start at 55 and keep the policy active until age 65. So, you have put in $40,000 in premiums if you start at age 25. And, if you start at 55, you might have to pay $20,000 in premiums for the same amount of insurance.

The key question is: what could you have done with the $40,000 in premiums that you put into the whole life insurance policy and what would you have with that money? As we stated earlier, the return you are likely to earn on these policies in 2021, is around 4–5%. This is obviously much higher than the other savings vehicles we've discussed earlier, but what about investments? See stocks below.

I've heard that once we have children, we absolutely need to buy insurance. Is that true?

First of all, a child doesn't need a life insurance policy. You should be able to pay for the extremely unlikely case that your child unfortunately dies. Parents need life insurance to pay for the needs of a child if both of them die at once, or if only one of you is working and that parent passes away, or if one of you is earning substantially more than the other and that parent dies.

We recommend this insurance coverage be term insurance. The rule of thumb is to buy about 7–8x the amount of annual before–tax income you want to replace. Of course, this really depends on the age of your child or children. If you have one child that is 16, getting a $1,000,000 policy is just too much. But if you have two children under 5, getting a $1,000,000 policy could be appropriate. On the www.360financialliteracy.org website, there is a calculator there that can help you assess your needs.

Should I buy term insurance, universal life, or a whole–life insurance policy?

Just as we are not licensed to manage your money, we are not licensed to sell you insurance. And this question is very difficult to answer since we don't have all your information. Some key questions that should be answered:

- Are you married? If so, does your spouse/partner make less or more than you?

- Do you have children or other dependents who would need income support if you were to die? If not, life insurance is likely unnecessary.

- What is your current savings level, in and out of retirement funds?

- What is your current income level?

- What is your current disposable income?

- How old are you?

- How old are your dependents? Even if you do have children, if they are already out of college and working, it's unlikely you need to have life insurance to ensure they have support.

I've heard that term insurance is like renting a home and buying cash value life insurance is like buying a home. If you buy a 20–year term, you have nothing at the end of the period, but with cash value you have money like the equity in your house. Is that true?

This is absolutely true. The issue is the return you will earn on the cash value insurance over the twenty years versus alternative investments.

What about Cryptocurrencies?

In recent years, cryptocurrencies have become a popular investment vehicle. Cryptocurrencies or crypto currencies or crypto (for short) is a digital asset which is supposed to work as a way to exchange products or services in which the records of the ownership of the individual coins are stored in an online ledger. This online ledger is stored in a database using complicated cryptography to ensure the transactions and the coins themselves are secure. These securities do not exist in physical form (thus the statement "digital asset") and no central bank has issued them. Bitcoin was the first cryptocurrency, originally released as open–source software in 2009. In early 2021, there were over 2,300 cryptos with value and over 2,500 currencies in total.

Bitcoin had the largest market capitalization at over $500 billion in early 2021 after the price of the heavily traded security more than tripled in just a few months.

Should you invest in Bitcoin or one of the other 2,300 cryptos? We suggest you both write down your levels of belief in each investment you are considering. Using a scale of one to ten, one being massive doubt, 10 being massive faith.

We suggest once you review your scales, invest if you both have a high belief level. We suggest that your scale should tend toward eight or above. What is your level of belief? What is your partner's? What is your livable solution?

Let's talk more about how fear plays a big part in investing. We have been taught by almost all financial services companies that as you get older, you should invest less in stocks and more in so–called less risky investments like bonds or cash.

First of all, how is 'less risky' defined? Usually, risk is defined by the volatility of the asset. How much it goes up or down in a particular period, a day or a month, a quarter or a year. As we noted above with CDs, another risk is generating an insufficient return because of risk aversion. Therefore, the risk is you outlive your assets.

But shouldn't it be defined as the risk of loss—the downside risk? Should we really care about 'upside risk'?

What is the probability of loss in bonds over the next five years (from 2021) given where the ten–year Treasury note is (approximately 0.7 percent)? Well, in the last fifty years, there has not been one instance of the note ending a year below 1%.

If the next five are anything like the time period before the financial crisis, then the probability of the ten–year Treasury note being higher is close to 100%. And the chance of you losing money in Treasury bonds or corporate bonds, which tend to follow the moves in Treasuries, is quite high.

Now, given that you know this, why would you "diversify" into an asset class that you *know* has a very high probability of losing money? When interest rates go up, the value of bonds goes down because you would just buy a new bond with the higher coupon rate rather than own the existing bond that yields less.

You would only invest in bonds if you feared that you would lose more in other asset classes, like stocks. So, it comes back to fear, and its siblings—worry and doubt!

Here is one story Joel heard growing up. Maybe you can relate:

Whenever someone ordered a Dr Pepper soda when he was out with his parents, his mother would ask his dad: "Remember when your dad had the chance to buy that stock right when it went public?

(Joel assumes this was at the IPO, or initial public offering price). That was such a big, missed opportunity. What would it be worth now?"

This sounds like a case of focusing on missed opportunities rather than realizing the many more lucrative windfalls. We call this negative reviewing. We always suggest remembering and focusing on the positive experiences and learning from the missed ones.

Actually, Dr Pepper went public in 1946 and was taken private in a leveraged buyout in 1984.

Let's talk about stocks and stock mutual funds.

One key question we get asked is: *Should I invest in mutual funds at all?*

To answer the question quickly, we believe you can do it all yourself. We do understand many of you just won't do it. And you will want to invest in stocks through funds.

We then highly recommend using passive management, not active. The difference is that passive management is investing in an index. That is, the fund simply replicates the index by investing in all five hundred stocks of the Standard and Poor's 500, if it is an S&P 500 fund. Or the index fund replicating the Dow Jones Industrial Average by investing in the thirty stocks in that index. And so on. Obviously, there are many different indices, including international funds, and there are even real estate, commodity, currency, and bond index funds.

Since the index funds just represent the overall index and are essentially run by computer programs, their expense ratio or cost to invest is very low. Generally, the S&P 500 index fund costs less than 0.2 percent, while many actively managed funds cost 2% or more. The result is that if you were to invest $100 a month in each fund and assume an 8 percent annual return in each, the difference, just because of the expenses, would be about $25,000 after twenty–five years. Wouldn't you prefer to have that in your pocket and not the fund companies?

There is a big assumption in the above example. It assumes that the returns of an actively managed fund and the passive fund are exactly the same. Of course, we know that less than one in four actively managed funds outperforms a passive fund over time. Thus, besides the expense hit, your return is likely to be lower than the average 8 percent return as well, if you invest in an actively managed mutual fund.

In his amazing *New York Times* best seller, *I Will Teach You To Be Rich*, Ramit Sethi explains that "All our lives, we've been taught to defer to experts: teachers, doctors, and investment 'professionals.' But ultimately, expertise is about results. In our culture of worshipping experts, what have the results been? When it comes to finances in America, they've been pretty dismal."

Sethi goes on to say that "financial experts—in fact, fund managers and anyone who attempts to predict the market—are often no better than amateurs. They're often worse. The vast majority of twenty–somethings can earn more than the so–called 'experts' by investing on their own, as we have seen recently with day trades. No financial adviser. No fund manager . . ."

Sethi goes on to state that "Most young people don't need a financial adviser . . . Plus, financial advisers don't always look out for your interests. They're supposed to help you make the right decisions about your money, but keep in mind that they're actually not obligated to do what's best for you. Some of them will give you very good advice, but many of them are pretty useless. If they're paid on commissions, they usually will direct you to expensive, bloated funds to earn their commissions."

We tell people if you are *not* interested in investing in the stock market, then find something you are interested in. It doesn't have to be shares that create your financial freedom. It could be rental income from real estate, or an Amazon fulfillment business or an EBay product fulfillment business. It could be developing a platform on

YouTube or a following on Instagram. It might be franchising or trading currencies or commodities. There are literally hundreds of ways to make money. The methods are only limited by your imagination. What about starting a YouTube channel and getting advertisers?

If you'd like to learn more about stock and DIY investing, Joel is giving away his 5–step proprietary stock screen to anyone who emails him at Joel@SaLaurMor.com.

Chapter 6 Exercise

Share with each other:

- What were you taught about bonds and stocks growing up?

- Growing up, what did you learn about investments?

  - Is "common knowledge" what you have gained from watching the talking heads on CNBC or Bloomberg or some other similar show? Or is it from what you learned by catching snippets from your parents talking to each other while you were growing up?

  - Or perhaps your friends' parents or your friends themselves?

Key Points from Chapter 6

- Term insurance is exactly what it sounds like. You have the insurance for a specific period of time or term. It can be 10 years or 20 years or more. Term insurance is pure insurance. You pay your monthly or annual premium and if you die before the period of time is up, your heirs or beneficiaries get the amount of the policy, also known as the face amount. There is no savings element here.

- A child doesn't need a life insurance policy. You should be able to pay for the extremely unlikely case that your child unfortunately dies. Parents need life insurance to pay for the needs of a child if both of them die at once, or if only one of you is working and that parent passes away, or if one of you is earning substantially more than the other and that parent dies.

- A fixed annuity is one in which you put in a lump sum or invest over time and the insurance company credits you an interest rate that is fixed based on their ability to invest in bonds and other investments.

- A variable annuity has a minimum crediting rate—currently less than 1%. This annuity invests in various types of mutual fund options and there is no guarantee that you will get that return.

- A Roth IRA is a special retirement account that you fund with post–tax income (you can't deduct your contributions on your income taxes). Once you have done this, all future withdrawals that follow Roth IRA regulations are tax–free. Because every penny you stash in a Roth IRA is your money, you can tap your contributions (but not your earnings on those contributions) at any time, tax–free and penalty–free. Please note you contribute to Roth IRAs outside a company retirement fund.

- Crypto is a digital asset which is supposed to work as a way to exchange products or services in which the records of the ownership of the individual coins are stored in an online ledger. These securities do not exist in physical form (thus the statement "digital asset") and no central bank has issued them. Bitcoin was the first cryptocurrency, originally released as open–source software in 2009. In early 2021, there were over 2,300 cryptos with value and over 2,500 currencies in total.

- If you are *not* interested in investing in the stock market, then find something you are interested in. It doesn't have to be shares that create your financial freedom. It could be rental income from real estate, or an Amazon fulfillment business or an EBay product fulfillment business. It could be developing a platform on YouTube or a following on Instagram. It might be franchising or trading currencies or commodities. There are literally hundreds of ways to make money.

CHAPTER 7:
DREAMS AND DESIRES

Back to our parable:

"He wants the sports car." The arbitrator announced as he walked in.

"I thought you said the car was yours," Natalie said as she turned her head to face me.

"It is mine...Well, I am not actually on the owner's note, but he bought it for me. I printed out the emails as proof. It is right here." I said shuffling to that section in the massive notebook I compiled. "If he wants it, he can have it." I said resigned. I was past caring.

"He bought you a car?" The arbitrator asked incredulously. I am guessing he saw him spew enough anger toward me that a gift of this magnitude seemed incongruous.

"Yes. And I never really wanted it. In fact, I was really upset that he bought it without discussing it with me."

"Tell me more," the arbitrator urged. I wasn't sure if he was sincere. I looked over at Natalie, who nodded. I could see the laugh she was trying to conceal. Clearly, she had read the email and now remembered the story.

"Well, about five years ago, I was back in school and struggling emotionally. A lot. The BMW Z3 had just come out. And it was cute as a button. I used to dream that I would have that lifestyle with the new job I would surely get after school. I had a great friend who bought me a matchbox version as a focus tool. Every time I was struggling, or exhausted, I would let it roll back and forth across my desk. He saw it when he was visiting once. And loved my story. So, he bought me the car."

"That was nice of him," said the surprised arbitrator.

"Actually, it was just another way he didn't hear me," I sighed. "When I told him the story of the matchbox car, I told him I didn't really ever want the actual car. It was a silly desire. Not

a real dream. I could have bought the car if I wanted. The real dream was the lifestyle. And as such, I traveled and I bought my condo. I told him all of this. And still, he went and sold the one car that he actually owned, to buy a car we would only use three months out of every year in Seattle. So, again, I say – if he wants it – let him have it. I was always upset that he bought it."

"Ah yes, but he bought it for you," he said pointing to the email Natalie handed him. "So, it is yours to do with as you please," said the arbitrator and left to tell him the news.

What did you dream about as a child?

Did you want to be a fireman? The President? A dancer? A pilot? A superhero?

What did you desire as a child? Did you want a new toy? A new bike?

What is the difference between dreams and desires? A dream is a vision of the bigger picture of what you want out of life, while a desire is a symbol of something more tangible that you might want in the shorter, more immediate term.

Did your dreams and desires change as you grew older? When? And why?

You may think that your childhood dreams and desires either had no basis in reality — wanting to be a superhero — or that they were simply impractical.

Consider:

- Did your dreams and desires change when life or finances got in the "way"? Or did they evolve as you learned more about yourself and the world?

- Did the dreams of saving the world or just pursuing joy go away?

- Why do you think that is?

- Do you believe there is a way to honor that now?

- How can your dreams and desires from childhood intersect with your dreams and desires of today?

For example, if you dreamed of being a superhero, what superhero action today would give you that same feeling?

Some ways to consider this include:

1. What about the superhero enthralled you? The fight for justice? Helping the underdog?

2. Now that you have defined the action, what can you do today that would give you the same elation? For example, if you wanted to be a superhero because you loved how they helped people, you can find a way to help people.

Discuss with your partner and decide how to honor your dreams from your childhood. Take a moment to make a plan to do so going forward.

Let's go back to our current dreams and desires:

- Can your dreams and desires intersect themselves?

- How do your actions feed your dream?

As a little child, all Mollie wanted to do was dance. The desire consumed her. She loved the movement, and even more, she was dancing with friends in sparkly tutus. She was sold!

But even as she pursued this desire with singular focus — oftentimes forgoing activities with friends for rehearsals or even just practice, her dad always reminded her that making a living as a dancer was not an option. It would never afford her the lifestyle she wanted.

Was this a good warning? Sure. Based on his own experiences, he was doing his best to set realistic goals and trying to teach her to develop her formal education alongside her creative one.

He did, after all, fund every one of those private classes, all the costumes, and all the trips. Did he kill her dream? No. He just widened her scope.

As Mollie met more dancers from around the world, and met more friends that traveled, she was intrigued. She would listen in wonder at their adventures. She would be entranced by the descriptions of the different places, the rich culture and often the places in the world that were a part of the dance.

And soon that became her dream: She wanted to see what the whole world had to offer. Her desire to dance remained.

Now, her dad's warning came into play – she didn't care what her job was. All that mattered was that she had the ability to travel to all the places she dreamed about. So, she pursued a career that would afford her the opportunity to make and save money. And when faced with a choice, she always preferred to save money so that she could add more funds to her travel account. That was her new desire. She aligned her desires with her daily actions and they fed her dreams.

Our dreams and desires are windows into the future of what "could be." They keep us going in life and they should always be honored. Remember, as Mike Dooley says in his bestseller, *Infinite Possibilities: The Art of Living Your Dreams*™, "We are not here just to survive, we are here to thrive." This objective can only be met by pursuing what stirs our heart.

As adults, we often feel like we have to separate our dreams from our desires. For example, Mollie may have dreamed of being a dance performer, but now her desire shifted from dance practice and rehearsals to wanting a steady paycheck.

As we grow, our dreams and desires may shift. Mollie's dream shifted towards traveling. And she, therefore, ensured that her career path was able to fund her dream to travel.

We may feel bogged down and tell ourselves that we cannot afford to have dreams because we have bills and responsibilities. Recall the lessons from the Ways to Save – Chapter 5. We absolutely can have responsibilities *and* dreams. One solution would be that you can put aside some money every week to fund your dreams. Be sure to have the conversation with your love on how to fulfill both of your dreams. It is of course, possible to have both and then have shared dreams too!

Consider the following Venn diagram.

You will have your dreams; your partner will have theirs. At some point, they will intersect. As a bonus, think of one dream you can work towards together (represented by the heart in the middle of the intersection).

**Please note: It is great to have interests outside of your relationship. First, it allows you both to have time to yourselves. Second, it helps you to develop as a person. Third, it brings perspective to your life. Last, having time away from each other is a form of loving yourself.

Hot Hint! Honor your dreams. Find a way to follow them. Bonus: Find one dream you can pursue together.

Follow your dream. Shoot for the stars!

- What are some consistent action steps/commitments you can make towards this dream?

- Solidify your plan. Set the day/date you will start and when you will evaluate your dream.

Do you think real life is too busy?

Does it feel like the "reality of life" is too busy to pay attention to your dreams and desires?

Are you too busy with the tasks at hand...be it the bills, kids, chores, errands, or work demands?

That happens to all of us. At some point in life, and even in our relationships, our primary goal goes from learning everything about ourselves and each other to settling into a routine. But what happens when the routine gets boring?

Statistically, the average person will change their career (not job — career) five to seven times. When you factor in the changes that come within each career — be it organizational or technology changes — we see that variety is what we crave.

But The Kids Need Me!

The demands of children are real. We often forgo our own dreams and desires because of their constant needs. Especially as new parents. And while that is normal, they need us to be whole people so we can raise them to be whole people.

The reality is, they need to be fed, the diapers need to be changed, and the list goes on. There is no down time. And yet, there has to be. As Esther Perel suggests in *Mating in Captivity*, we should take a lesson from our kids. They train us with their cries, tantrums and demands. In turn, we potty train them, teach them to eat their vegetables, get them to sleep at certain times. We must take back even one hour for ourselves and one hour for your union. Have that dream. Think about your desires — for your partner and yourself.

A fun activity you can do together to help focus you towards any of these goals is to create a visual that you can both see. You can create:

- A Vision Board; A vision board is a visual representation of your dreams and desires. Choose your favorite images and paste them to a board.

- A list — this can be on the fridge, the bathroom mirror — or anywhere you can both see it; or

- Chalkboard paint on a door.

Joint dreams to consider:

- Try donating time to a cause you both are interested in. Mollie and her husband joined the Big Brothers, Big Sisters of Atlanta and mentored a sister and a brother. It was a great way to mentor, give back to their community, and bond over their experiences.

- Try new hobbies. A couple we know tries a new hobby every year. One year it was beekeeping. One year it was dancing. Either way, they get to spice up their lives with a new endeavor – together.

- Keep in mind, you may not love everything you try. The point isn't to love everything, it is to try.

Remember, dream. Then dream bigger.

Chapter 7 Exercises

Exercise 1

Talk about your dreams.

As you go through this, please keep in mind:

- Learning your past helps you understand your present and adjust as needed.

- Sharing your dreams and desires from your childhood and as you grew up helps your partner understand you and learn more about you, perhaps even what moti-vates you today.

- Our dreams honor our childhood; they help bring that spirit and energy back to our lives.

- The dreams and desires from our childhood play into our present–day lives.

- Finding ways to honor our dreams and desires helps us to create meaning in your life today.

Share!

- What were your dreams as a child?

- Why was this your dream? Give all the details you can recall.

- What were your dreams as a teen or as a young adult?

- What caused the shift from childhood dream to your teen or your young adult dream?

- Now, share, what two things you learned about your partner.

Exercise 2

Discuss with each other.

- Are you aligned with your dreams and actions?

- How do you and your partner sync up?

- Is it ok for you and your partner to have different dreams and desires?

Our answer is yes, it is...the goal would be to find a way to honor both of you.

Exercise 3

Share with each other.

- Explore your own intersections between the dreams and desires of your childhood to the ones of today.

- What is your current dream? Why?

- What is your current desire? Why?

- Do your dreams and desires intersect? If so, how?

- If not, what can you do to come into alignment?

Please note: Your individual dreams and desires do not have to intersect with your partner's dreams and desires. However, respecting and supporting each other is necessary for you and your partner. And respecting each other's dreams and desires are necessary for your union.

- How do your dreams and desires match up with your childhood dreams and desires? Are there any connections?

96

- How do your dreams and desires match up with your young adult dreams and desires? Are there any connections?

- What are three dreams for the future (5+ years)?

- What are you doing today to achieve any one of those dreams?

- What can your partner do to help you achieve those dreams?

- Where do you both intersect with your individual dreams and desires?

Don't worry about funding these dreams at this moment. The idea is to dream and realize that you can take baby steps toward them today. Also, do not worry if your dreams and desires are different from your partner's. The idea is to build a relationship where you both are helping each other achieve your dreams and then to dream bigger.

Exercise 4

Discuss

- How do your dreams and desires match up?

- Can they co–exist? How?

- How can you support each other in your dreams?

Now let's talk about your dreams as a couple. This is the "we" portion of your dreams and desires. This is where you both get to define what you want and how to come together to make it what you both want. When you are building something — anything — it is always better to share the vision of what you are building rather than to build separately. Define your dreams individually. Later you will be given space to share with each other.

Journal Individually

Yours:

- What does a weekday in your dream life look like?

- What does a weekend in your dream life look like?

- What does your dream home look like?

- What does your dream vacation look like?

- What does your dream savings look like?

- What does your dream retirement look like?

- What other goals, dreams and desires do you have?

Discuss, Dream, and Plan together

- Where do you both intersect?

- How can you honor both sets of your dreams?

- Or do you love your partner's dreams so much that they are now yours too?

Journal Together

Ours:

- What does a weekday in our dream life look like?

- What does a weekend in our dream life look like?

- What does our dream home look like?

- What does our dream vacation look like?

- What does our dream savings look like?

- What does our dream retirement look like?

- What other goals, dreams and desires do we have?

Find a dream you can pursue together. You can choose to use one of yours or your partner's dreams, or you can find a new dream. Pursuing something together gives you another point of connection and helps to continue to create shared meaning.

Think of something you both like...and start simple. Simple dreams help you to put together a plan that you can pursue in a straightforward manner.

When Mollie and her husband first started doing this, they began with what would appear to look like a chore: walking the dog. They did this once a week together. They converted one of their daily chores into a weekly connection point for the both of them. Then, a few years later, it grew into a week–long hike in Spain.

Key Points from Chapter 7:

- Align your desires to support your dreams.

- Yours and your partner's dreams and desires can both be supported.

- Dream, then dream bigger.

CHAPTER 8:
DREAMS AND DESIRES SUPPLEMENTAL SECTION

Mollie: When I was in second grade, my teacher brought in a guest speaker to talk to us about our dreams. He started by asking us what our dream car would be. It was split down the traditional gender lines. Many of the boys said their dream car was the same one their dad or favorite uncle had. Many of the girls said their dream car was the one their mom had. A few kids wanted cars they saw their favorite actors driving. I wanted the car I saw around in my neighborhood. It has been more than 40 years, and I can still remember the days I would see it driving around. It was an older Rolls Royce. It was stunning pearl white and had brown accents. And it just looked regal. I was not into cars, but that one, I learned about.

Our guest speaker explained that our dream car represented the dream we thought we could achieve. He also explained that whether we were looking in at our own life – i.e., to family for inspiration, or outside – i.e., neighbors or TV, we could still dream bigger.

But how do we do that? How do we activate that part of our imagination?

Are you overwhelmed by your current circumstances? By the number of choices? Or have you just achieved one dream and not sure what to dream about now?

You can open your eyes and your heart. It isn't as easy as it sounds. In fact, I know it is hard. But I also know it is possible. So, how do you open up when you feel closed?

- You take time for yourself.
  - Meditate
  - Relax
  - Take a bath
  - Let your mind wander so that you have fresh eyes to look at...well, everything!

- You commit to trying something new.
  - ○ Try one tiny thing a day
  - ○ Or endeavor a new skill for 3 months. Do you still like it? Keep going for a year. Do you love it? What inspires you about it?
    - ▪ Mollie tried learning Spanish for 3 months. She used an app on her phone and she was inspired. So, she stuck to it for 18 months. Now, she looks forward to traveling so she can use her new skill.
- You can commit to helping someone.
  - ○ Helping others is a great way to open your heart and inspire you to greater things.

So, how did Mollie dream bigger? She took some time to think outside of the one shiny pretty car and thought about her dad's car – a dependable Volvo, and her brother's car – a sports car. And she thought about that pretty car. And she figured – why choose? If she was going to dream, she might as well dream really big. So, she figured she would have all three. And when she shared this tidbit with one of her aunts, her aunt tried to tell her that it was not possible. But Mollie told her she would do it. Her aunt responded with, "I know you will."

As Mollie mentioned, she is not a car person. But she does live a life where she feels like she has a dream life. She takes these types of vacations every year. One family style vacation, one adventure, and one luxury. So, now how does she dream bigger?

She continues to learn. She continues to be in service.

What about you?

If you can put everything aside, and dream, what do you want? What life do you want? Put aside logic, thoughts of bills, and responsibilities, and dream. Then dream bigger.

Take a moment to discuss with your partner.

CHAPTER 9:
DIFFERENCES

There are many different schools of thought on how to assess and deal with your differences as a couple. We will say, whichever one works best for you is the best one. With that being said, we also firmly believe that no matter what your differences are, there is always a way to respect and, even celebrate them.

Differences are what attracts us to our partner, but those same differences can also be the things that drive us crazy later in the relationship. This chapter will dive into your differences and help you find a way to respect the differences you both have and love each other even more.

When Mollie was a young child of just 12, her dad took her to the bank and helped her open her first bank account. It was a rite of passage for sure. In vivid detail, she can recall the moment that she signed that signature card. She was sitting there contemplating the signature that would define and follow her through life. She felt the heady weight of the moment.

She was young, and knew she was young. And yet, she felt ready for this moment. After all, she had earned this money. It was money from dance performances. The act of having this account, seeing her name on it, forecast her following years.

She learned what checking accounts were — compared to savings accounts. Later in high school, when she was learning about the stock market, she dreamed about how much more she could earn compared to the rate on her savings account. When she talked to her dad about her ideas and the stocks she had researched, he was completely against the idea.

He feared the losses that can occur in the stock market. He was clearly The Protectionist Type. Any dabbling he had done in the stock market "always" ended up in a loss. Mollie had learned that while dips occur, the overall long–term trajectory was upward. Mollie and her dad had a fundamental difference of opinion. She thought of it as an investment whereas her dad thought of it as a gamble. And, since she was just 15, there was not much action she could take. Around the same time, her uncle, her very successful uncle, started asking her how school was, and what she was learning. So, she told him about the stock market play money they were investing at school. His opinions of the stock market were very different than her dad's opinions.

Mollie's uncle used funds he did not mind losing. He chose to ride out the downturns. Mollie learned a valuable lesson here. First, that differences exist. One was not right over the other – they were just different, based on experiences. Much like we learned in the Financial Backgrounds chapter, we are shaped by our experiences. These experiences created different risk tolerance levels within her dad and uncle. Second, she learned that these differences can co–exist.

So, what is Risk Tolerance?

Simply put, risk tolerance is the tolerance any person has with the amount of risk they are taking. For example, are you comfortable investing in the stock market or do you prefer a standard savings account? Below are detailed explanations of Low, Medium, and High Risk Tolerances.

Low: Someone with low risk tolerance does not want to lose money and thus will favor investments (savings accounts) that have a low likelihood of losing money. People with low risk tolerance prefer certificates of deposit (CDs) and Treasury bills (T–bills) to stocks and real estate.

Medium: Someone with medium risk tolerance is willing to lose some money but not much. They will prefer investments that have a relatively low probability of losing money. They will invest in stocks but only those that pay dividends and dividends that have been increasing year after year. They will invest in life insurance policies instead of checking and savings accounts and CDs.

High: Someone with high risk tolerance is willing to risk losing money to get potentially much better results. People with high risk tolerance prefer stocks and real estate to CDs and T–bills.

An aggressive investor, or one with a high risk tolerance, is willing to risk losing money to get potentially better results. A conservative investor, or one with a low risk tolerance, favors investments that maintain his or her original investment.

Opposites Attract; Like Attracts Like

Wait, what?? Which one is right? Actually, both are right. The fact is that we are different. After all, we come from different families and different backgrounds. Recall the differences of Mollie's dad and her uncle. And no matter how different we are, there is something about us that resonates with our partner, which ultimately means we have some similarities *and* differences – and we appreciate both in our partner. We click with our partner; it might be one thing, or it might be several. The important question is: how do we deal with the differences that are a reality in our relationship?

Dealing with Differences

As a clarification, we are not referring to conflict when we talk about differences. Differences are not the same as conflicts. Conflicts are more intense; fueled with emotions. Conflicts will be discussed in the next chapter.

When considering differences, one of the first things to consider is to gain an understanding of what contributes to the difference. Recall the 'Why' in your answers. Another consideration is to ponder what the wish is behind your stance.

Some differences are easier to evaluate and handle. Let's start with what looks like a simple example. We suggest multiple savings accounts. We also like naming them "Emergency," "Vacation," "Gifts," etc. However, some prefer fewer accounts. The difference is easy to spot, understand, and even come to a compromise. So, what do you do? Compromise.

Hot Hint! Consider keeping two extra accounts, one for emergencies, and one for fun. It is the same amount of money, just fewer accounts.

But how do you deal with bigger differences? More important differences such as:

- Should we borrow on our credit card to pay for our next vacation?

- How much do we actually save per paycheck?

- How much do we put away for retirement?

- What does our vacation fund look like? Is vacation important?

- What is our risk tolerance?

Let's consider how much to save per paycheck. Once you factor in all of your bills, what do you have left? Do you want to put all of it in savings? Or leave a little wiggle room for a dinner out or that special bottle of wine? First, if that is something you want, we suggest adding that to your budget. Second, after considering your weekly and monthly bills, ask each other how much you want to put towards your retirement accounts and how much you want to put towards emergency funds or fun funds.

Now, let's consider what happens if one partner has more tolerance for risk than the other. You will need to ask yourselves if there is a compromise to be reached. If considering an investment account, perhaps consider being more risk tolerant with a percentage of that account. For example, maybe 30% aggressive, and the remainder moderate? Again, go through the questions listed above and decide what feels right and comfortable for you both.

Next, consider, if this is a new difference, or did you or your partner always feel this way? If it is a new difference, what is the story that fuels this? This last question can apply to a lot of topics. You will find a wide range of differences to consider in Mollie's book, *Infinitely Loving: A Workbook to Support Couples in Creating a Life of Love Together.* Over time, the answers to these questions are subject to change. And you may need to revisit and answer them again and again. Your growth together should enhance this ongoing dialog. It is that mutual understanding of the dream behind what we want, that will lead to a deepening of the friendship and the relationship.

Hot Hint! If you and your partner have wildly differing viewpoints on something, do not assume that you can change their mind. The goal of this chapter is to find common ground within your financial differences.

Not everyone comes into a relationship having discussed and solved all money topics, let alone the key issues. That is why we are here to help you. And, as we go through life events, circumstances, aging, and as health and other changes occur in our lives, who and what we are, will continue to change. We will adapt, grow and modify. Just as we learn about our partners and ourselves as we did previously through learning the stories of each other's lives, our differences also bring valuable teaching and learning tools for us.

Hot Hint! If you try to chase two rabbits, you won't catch either one. You need to pick which rabbit you want to chase.

For example, you cannot save every penny, and allow for financial flow in your life. However, there is a way to find common ground; a way to integrate these differences into our lives, cherish them and celebrate them. By learning how to examine the difference, learn about why we think the way we do, and to share these with our partner, we continue to enhance our growth and the growth of our relationship.

Cherish your differences. They are as important as your similarities. To make the most of your relationship, we recommend first honoring yourself as an individual and consider what experiences fed your Money Personality Type. Then think of your partner as an individual themselves. Finally, consider your union as an entity unto itself. Of course, there will be a point where you and your partner become the "we." After all, you both are greater than the sum of your parts. That said, it is imperative to remember that you are each still your own person unto yourselves. Love each other for who you are. Not for the potential person you can become. Cherish each other as you want to be cherished and grow from there. After all, you are perfect just as you are.

Chapter 9 Exercises

Exercise 1

Answer and discuss the following questions.

We ask 'Why' after each question with the intention to have you both explain the story behind your answer. Be sure to offer details and anecdotes from your past to facilitate a deeper understanding.

- What is your preferred mode of savings?

- Why?

- What is your ideal amount in the bank?

- Why?

- What is your comfortable risk tolerance – moderate, or high?

- Why?

Exercise 2

When it comes to differences, consider, what is your wish, your desire, your want, and your needs in the specific difference being considered in the following:

- Why do we want to have more in savings?

- Why should we have individual, multiple accounts, or both?

- Why is your risk tolerance what it is?

- What is the dream behind what you want? What is your longing?

- What is the dream behind what your partner wants, assuming it is different from what you want?

Exercise 3

Review your history with each other:

- What is the history behind those stances for each of you?

- Are you used to emergencies?

- Are you unaccustomed to saving for fun activities?

- What about the dreams behind your stances?

Find your common ground on what feels right and comfortable for you both.

Exercise 4

List out three topics you want to cover. For example, how much to save per paycheck, how often do we vacation and what is our budget, and how much do we save for retirement? You can use the three we suggest or use any three financial questions that you desire.

- What is your stance? Is it different from your partner's?

- What is the history behind each of your stances?

- Is there a dream behind those stances?

- How does your history affect your dream behind those stances?

- Can you find common ground?

The goal is not necessarily to find agreement; rather to understand what is truly important and to find what satisfies <u>both</u> of your feelings about the difference.

What part of the difference is truly important, and what part can you let go of?

Hot Hint! It comes down to what is the concept or the dream behind the difference.

Exercise 5

Recall, in Chapter 2, we took inventory of your backgrounds and beliefs. In the following exercise, you will review each of the following and consider what history and what dream lies within each of these topics.

Consider the words in the table.

Money	Retirement	Insurance
Cash	Travel/Vacation	Kid's College
Credit	Taxes	Bank Loans
Personal Loans	Earnings	Inheritance
Investments	Interest Rates	Emergency Expense

The goal of this exercise is to review why we think what we think. It is especially helpful when we see our differences as they relate to our history. It helps us understand each other even better.

Instructions: This is great as a conversation, and even better when you write it down and work on the answers together. This way, when you revisit the exercises in a year or five, you can see how things have shifted for each of you, and as a couple.

- One by one, discuss your story with each of the words in the chart above.

- What do you feel?

- What is your dream behind the meaning of the word?

- How does your definition differ from your partner's?

- Is there a livable understanding you can come to? Or a change you can make?

- What else can give you this feeling?

- Will the shift give you what you seek? Explain.

Key Points from Chapter 9

- Differences exist. One is not right over the other. They were just different based on experiences. And these differences can co–exist.

- No matter how different we are, there is something about us that resonates with our partner, which ultimately means we have some similarities and some differences – and we can appreciate both in our partner.

- The important point is to find common ground; to understand what is truly important: to find what satisfies your feelings about the difference.

- If you and your partner have wildly differing viewpoints on something, do not assume that you can change their mind. Find common ground within your differences.

- To make the most of your relationship, we recommend first honoring yourself as an individual, then each other as individuals, and then your union as an entity unto itself.

CHAPTER 10:
CONFLICT

"Underneath every complaint is a longing." – John Gottman

We have told you quite a tale about a couple in deep conflict. Many of the issues were about finances. And many of the other issues we did not discuss came about because of finances. Ultimately, money is one of the biggest issues in any relationship. Consult any relationship expert or article, and you will find that finances are either the number one reason or the number two reason why couples have conflict and ultimately break up. But did it have to go that far for this couple? Of course not. Conflict is not inherently bad. The magic is in the recovery process. So, how could this couple have stayed together and still recovered from their financial woes? All the couple needed was to have some open conversations about money. This chapter will help you find ways to do just that.

The first thing they would have had to do was to realize that money is linked to emotions. In fact, consider the previous chapters in this book and you will see exactly what goes into any conflict:

1. Your Money Personality Type

2. Your Financial Background

3. Your Emotions around money

4. Your Dreams and Desires around money

5. Your Savings perspective

6. Your Differences

As you consider your conflicts, consider those chapters and the lessons you have learned about each other. You are not searching for perfection in your partner or even yourself. You are looking for progress.

"You don't love someone because they're perfect, you love them in spite of the fact that they're not." – Jodi Picoult, best-selling author of more than 25 books.

Now that we know what feeds our perspectives on conflicts, here are 5 key causes of major financial conflicts:

1. Mismatched priorities – Whether you have a difference of opinion on how to save, what type of savings, or how aggressively you want to invest, when you are not clear about your priorities and why those are your priorities, it can lead to major disturbances in your relationship.

    a. We recommend considering:

        1. Your money personality types; and

        2. Your financial backgrounds and beliefs about your priorities.

        3. Talking to each other using some of the techniques detailed further on in this chapter.

2. Mismatched beliefs – Oftentimes we have different beliefs about what is an appropriate amount of credit, or what the right amount to give in personal and charitable gifts, and how much to spend on vacation. There are, of course, a whole host of other things as well.

    a. When it comes to discussing mismatched beliefs on finances, we suggest the following:

        i. When you are calm, sit down with your partner and talk about your belief system (recall the Financial Backgrounds chapter – Chapter 2) and create a budget.

3. Financial infidelity – Infidelity of any kind is not conducive to a trusting relationship. Financial infidelity is when you hide or lie to your partner about your spending. This can derail many of the plans you have worked out together and can eventually break you financially – as well as your relationship.

    a. We suggest:

        i. Create a budget and allot for your whims; and

        ii. Discuss openly any additional expenditures.

4. Mismatched budgets – From set budgets to impulse buys, if you have fundamentally different ideas about money, and how to handle money, it can cause some major issues in your relationship. As we learned in the previous chapter, differences are understandable. You came from different experiences and have different perspectives of said experiences.

    a. We suggest you review your financial goals with your Financial Backgrounds notes nearby. Offer respect and understanding as you make a plan to move forward in your finances. And do so with love.

5. Lack of planning – "Failing to plan is a plan to fail." – Alan Lakein, bestselling author of *How to Get Control of Your Time and Your Life*. Whether you had a plan that was working, that wasn't working, or didn't have one, you are here now. Take a moment and revel in that. Now, if you haven't made a plan, make one.

    a. How much do you want to save for your retirement?

    b. For a vacation?

    c. For your kid's college?

    d. For your parent's elder care?

    e. For your elder care?

    f. And don't forget emergencies.

    g. We suggest sitting down and creating a plan. Also, consider revisiting that plan quarterly or bi–annually to re–assess as needed.

When there is a misunderstanding or an imbalance of emotions, it is normal to feel upset. Emotions like these can be uncomfortable and messy – especially when it feels like some or all of these emotions are aimed at you. However, taking a deep breath and knowing how to deal with them will help you and your relationship.

Conversation is key and these kinds of conversations can be difficult. Plus, it is often tough to initiate difficult conversations. It takes trust and practice.

We are here to help you start these conversations regarding emotions that are uncomfortable and that may seem aimed at you. Always remember to be honest and gentle and remember that you are on the same team.

Recall: You should not be afraid of conflicts. They are a normal part of relationships. They lead to growth. The true magic lies in your repair process. As part of your restoration process, you are given the opportunity to ask for what you need or want as part of dealing with the conflict.

Hot Hint! Focus on what you like. Don't focus on what you don't like, as it will continue to bring that into your life. This is how the Law of Attraction works. Ask for what you need or want from your partner – just be certain to make your requests with love.

One of the benefits that comes from conflict is that it leads to growth and deeper understanding of yourself and your partner. Be patient with your partner and yourself. Dealing with conflict is a learned process.

Has it happened to you that you felt your partner was being unreasonable when they were upset? While that may be true in the moment, it also holds true that your partner is, in fact, upset about something. Often, it isn't what they are saying. A little detective work and some understanding goes a long way to being supportive of your partner. Understanding also aids in averting and repairing conflicts.

So, let's practice! Below, we will review an example of a conflict.

Conflict: I want to go to Iceland in the winter. My husband wants to go somewhere warm.

- Were you both in conflict over the same thing? Yes.

  ○ Sometimes when we are in conflict, couples are actually fighting two different fights. Is that what happened with you? No.

- Take a moment and consider, what are each of you longing for? I want to see the Northern Lights. My love wanted to relax in warm weather.

- What was the dream behind the longing? I was dreaming of excitement and adventure. My love was dreaming of rest and relaxation.

- What was the outcome? We both felt heard, understood, and honored.

- Did you find a way to honor both of your longings? Yes.

- What is your livable solution? We decided to see the Northern Lights one year, with some relaxation days built in. And the next vacation, my love gets to decide.

- Armed with your new understanding, is there a change in your perception of the conflict? If so, what is the change? Yes, there was a change. We both learned what we each wanted on our time off. I want to make sure my love enjoys the vacation as much as I do. So, we will plan for some relaxation times in a resort in Iceland. That way we both enjoy that trip.

What can you do next time to avoid the conflict? We can talk to each other before we get mad. We can ask what we are looking for in the situation. We can ask questions.

Adding Love to Conflict

Here's an example:

Suppose you come home from a long day at work and the dishes are piled up in the sink. You're tired from your long day at work. You just battled traffic to come home and now you have unpleasant chores to tackle.

Please do not shortcut yourself out of a full conversation. Before getting too upset, consider asking your partner how they are feeling. Jumping to any conclusion is detrimental to the health of your relationship. Sometimes we think we are on the same page and that we have both read every email and text we each sent, but that is not always the case. Take a moment, say hello, and share some love. Then, share the details of your day. Finally, share the details of your current situation/irritation – if it's still a factor after your conversation.

Mollie's aunt used to tell her a story about conflicts and how to handle them. Mollie used to think this was her favorite story to tell new couples because she and Mollie's uncle famously never argued. Ever. And apparently, they are not alone. There is a small percentage of couples out there that never argue. But for the rest of us mere mortals who are in the majority, we will share the story of Mollie's aunt and what we eventually learned from it.

The Gypsy and the Pill

One day a gypsy came to town and was reported to have solutions to cure every issue – both physical and emotional. A lady in town was eager to see her. She was sure she had the worst issue of all – a husband who would fight with her every day. She loved him dearly and just wanted him to stop fighting with her. So, when this gypsy came to town, the lady was the first in line to see her. She told the gypsy everything. The gypsy gave her some pills with very specific instructions including how they needed to melt slowly in her mouth for best effect. Whenever her husband started to fight with her, *she* needed to take one pill. The lady was completely confused. This was supposed to be a cure for her husband – how was it going to work if *she* is the one who takes the pill??

The gypsy assured her that the instructions given were absolutely correct. So, the lady went home and as soon as her husband started to fight with her, she took a pill. And lo and behold, it worked! He stopped fighting with her! So, the next time he started to fight with her, she took a pill again. And it worked again! And the pill worked again and again, until she was out of pills. Now, she could not wait for the gypsy to come back to town. She drove over a hundred miles to see her to get a refill. But when she finally saw the gypsy, the gypsy laughed and told the lady it was only a salt pill. The pills were just so salty and dehydrating that they rendered the lady speechless. It kept her mouth shut and gave her time to collect her thoughts to talk to her husband rather than to fight with her beloved.

Mollie has heard this story many times. And when she first heard it, she thought her aunt was telling her not to argue. But then she realized, she was actually telling her the following:

- Don't be reactive.

- Timeouts are necessary.

- Don't meet anger with more anger.

Remember, do not worry and do not be concerned: conflicts happen. In fact, they are actually good and healthy for your relationship. It is how you work through and recover from them that will build or break your relationship.

Instead of the wife eating the salt pill, or being reactive and getting upset with her husband, she could stop to ask questions. For example, she could ask why he is upset. After all, those daily fights could be out of habit as much as the result of a bad day. Arresting the cycle only takes one person.

Hot Hint! When in conflict, don't assume...don't jump to conclusions. This can have an adverse effect on the situation; potentially making the matter worse.

Note: How we talk to each other matters. The Law of Attraction is always in play. When we talk with love, love comes back. When we talk with anything other than love, that too returns. The gift we are given is that we can arrest the cycle at any time and find a way to talk with love.

Dr. Gottman, the Best–selling author of *The 7 Principles that Make a Marriage Work*, says: "There are two views to every conflict and both are valid."

Chapter 10 Exercises

Exercise 1

Answer the following together.

- What was your most recent financial conflict?
  - Were you both in conflict over the same thing?
  - Sometimes when we are in conflict, couples are actually fighting two different fights. Is that what happened with you?

- If this happened with you, what were each of you upset about?

- Take a moment and consider, what are each of you longing for?

- What was the dream behind the longing?

- What was the outcome?

- Can you find a way to honor both of your longings?

- What is your livable solution?

- Armed with your new understanding, is there a change in your perception of the conflict? If so, what is the change?

- What can you do next time to avoid the conflict?

Exercise 2

Review a minor incident together.

Example:

- Minor Situation: I came home and the sink was full of dishes after a hard day and a traffic jam.

- How you handled it: I was exasperated and pissed off as I loaded the dishwasher.

- What was the outcome: I felt worse! We argued about me not being patient and him not helping with the housework. It was hours before we calmed down.

- What would you change: I would have ignored the dishes. If I had asked him how he was doing, I would have found out that he had received bad news. We would have connected over dinner. We would have done the dishes together.

Your turn. Discuss together. Each partner should pick one circumstance. Recall a minor incident that went awry. Then discuss what each of you could have done differently.

Minor situation 1:
How you handled it:
What was the outcome:
What would you change:

Minor situation 2:
How you handled it:
What was the outcome:
What would you change:

Tip: Remember to separate the incident from your partner. Every disturbance is not the end of the world. We suggest using code words, "ouch" and "that stung," or even ask "Are you ok?"

or "Why are you cranky?" or something benign that works for you.

For example, when Mollie's love comes home especially cranky (one of their code words), she stops to consider why he might be cranky, rather than to react to what is obviously not a normal conversation. If he can catch himself, he will apologize. If he is more than cranky, they will call a timeout.

<u>Your Turn</u>:

Discuss together:

Your code word(s) for showing you are hurt:

Your code word(s) for suggesting your partner is not in a good head space:

Exercise 3

Think back to the story about the Gypsy and the Pill. Discuss the following with each other:

- What is the woman's complaint?

- What do you think the woman is longing for?

- Do you see it differently than your partner? If so, can you see your partner's point of view?

We ask for your individual interpretations of this story, because we all interpret situations — both our own and other's — from our own perspective.

Key Points from Chapter 10:

- Conflicts are not inherently bad. The magic is in the recovery.

- Money is linked to emotions. Take time to consider each other as you move forward in your conversation.

- Remember your salt pill. Take time to listen to your partner. Take time to express your feelings and point of view as well. Remind each other of your backgrounds and backstory. This helps you understand each other as you move forward.

CHAPTER 11:
RECOVER AND
RESOLVE

As we have mentioned before, conflicts are not bad. It is how you recover from them that matters. The couple we have followed throughout this book had conflicts. Surely, we have all had some variation of those same conflicts. But they never found a way to come back to each other. They didn't find a way to understand each other's point of view. This chapter will review some techniques to help you recover – with love.

Two Loves and a Wish

Ask for a change. When you are both in a calm state. Ask for a change or a different approach. When asking for change, we suggest offering two loves and a wish. Start off by reminding your partner, that this conflict is not bigger than your love affair; that this conflict is not bigger than your relationship; that you appreciate your partner and their viewpoint.

Start with "two loves." This is where you state two things you appreciate about your love and then, ask for "one wish." This is the one thing that you'd like to see happen. Try this as a way to communicate your wishes with your partner.

Example:

Issue: My husband and I like to go out, but he does not want to go out as much as I do. He wants more quiet time, whereas I want more social activity.

Two loves and a wish: Honey, I respect how hard you work at your job (love). And I love that you enjoy your work so much (love). I would like to go out. Can we plan for at least one day a week that we go out and socialize (wish)?

*Please note that the 'loves' are sincere and apropos to the discussion.

Handling A Minor Disagreement

When handling a minor situation, before letting it go too far, we suggest starting with your A's. Triple A's, in fact: <u>Ask, Acknowledge, Ask</u>. This is the technique used in the dishes example above.

Example:

Ask what is wrong. "Hey honey, is everything ok with you?"

— After listening

Acknowledge the issue: "That sounds awful. What I heard was…"

<insert your understanding <u>in your own words</u> of the situation>

Then, discuss potential solutions <u>if appropriate</u>. Keep in mind, not everyone is looking for a solution. Sometimes your partner may only want to vent.

Ask for what you need. "I'm glad you shared that. Let's make sure we talk about all of our challenges as well as the good stuff."

Please remember:

- With both minor and more intense conflicts, do more than ask for change…tell your partner what is right and good about them and what they do for you!

- When asking for any change, it is always best to be kind and polite. You would want the same.

- As Mary Poppins said, "A spoonful of sugar helps the medicine go down." This is why the two loves and a wish technique works so well.

- Remember, the Law of Attraction. The more you appreciate your partner, the more you will see how much you have to appreciate!

- Describe the behavior, do not accuse, or label the person.

Describe how the behavior made you feel. Offer clear suggestions on what you need. For example, instead of "You're selfish," consider saying "When you don't include me, I feel left out."

Some things to do during intense conflicts:

- Take a break. Call a timeout. Studies evaluating human physiology show that a 20–minute break actually brings your heart rate down, reduces blood pressure and brings down elevations in various stress–related chemicals. But make sure you are not stewing, reliving the incident, or planning a rebuttal while you are taking your break. Take an actual break from each other's presence and the incident.

- Changing the topic, ignoring or sweeping something under the rug, doesn't help – after your break, come back and have the discussion with love.

- Look for something positive. It is impossible to hold a negative thought in your head at the same time as a positive one.

- Meditate, exercise, or do breathing exercises, read a book, or walk the dog. Do anything that takes your mind off the conflict.

- Take responsibility for your own feelings. If you are having a bad day, don't blame your partner for your bad mood/day/situation.

Once you have calmed down:

- Check in with yourself. What are you really upset about?

- Are your feelings hurt? Are you hungry? Tired? Frustrated?

- Is it your partner that upset you? If so, look beyond the words!

Why is a break important?

Just as the wife in the gypsy story learned to curb her retorts, it is imperative to speak gently to one another – especially when it comes to money. When we speak with anger, there are certain characteristics that show up that are not truly representative of how we feel toward one another, such as sarcasm or negativity.

When we approach our loved one with pent–up anger or frustration, we may not realize the effect of our explosiveness. This may trigger our partner to respond in kind or to become defensive. After all, the Law of Attraction is always at play. Eventually, that can work against our connection to one another and breeds contempt.

Not all of us have access to the gypsy and her magic salt pill. Instead – as described – take a breath, a break, and some time to regroup. Then come back to your partner and offer insights about your feelings.

I feel...A solution

To resolve the major conflicts, use the "I feel, a solution..." method. The first part involves calmly describing the situation, and actively listening. Then offering a solution.

1. Partner 1: describes how they feel and, if reasonable, offer insights for why they are upset. Remember to own your feelings using words like, "I feel..." or "It hurts my feelings when..."

   1. Use three adjectives to identify how you feel.

   2. Describe the incident – do not assign attributes to your partner.

   3. For example, "I feel hurt, left out, unimportant when you bought drinks for everyone you work with without talking to me."

2. Partner 2: Should actively listen. Try to hear the feelings behind the words. And try to hear the words not being said. Note: **This does not mean that you are agreeing with what your partner is saying. Rather, it is a means to bear witness to their feelings and to empathize with your partner.

3. Partner 2: Do not get defensive, and do not try to fix the issue. Defending your actions can make your partner feel like their feelings do not matter — and jumping in with a solution can inadvertently imply that you do not think your partner is smart enough to fix the issue themselves. And, after all, it might well have been inappropriate for your partner to join in the after–work drinks – and they may know that – but may just have been feeling down. Perhaps they just wanted to vent or process their feelings. Using your own words, repeat what you hear – and didn't hear. For example, "I heard you say you feel upset, insignificant, and left behind when I did not invite you to have drinks with my friends after work."

4. Partner 1: If your partner got it right, move on to the solution. If not, start over until you feel understood. Try to find a new way to gently tell your partner what you're feeling.

   Notes:

   **As you go through this process, you may find that sometimes you are upset about two different things. This is ok. As long as you are both heard and feel understood in the end.

   **If there are multiple issues, discuss one at a time. Realizing that sometimes we are reactive and creating an issue rather than eating our salt pill is taking ownership of our part in the moment.

   **As each person relays their feelings, hold each other's hands and look into each other's eyes. This changes the energy in the room to a loving space for you both. And this is your chance to hold each other's love in your hands and show you are connected to them and their feelings.

5. Now it is your partner's turn. Go through steps 1–5 with the roles reversed. Do both of you feel heard and understood? If so, move forward.

6. Plan to do it better next time. Propose a solution.

- For example, "I know it would have been inappropriate for me to join your work buddies, but I really needed a drink. Perhaps you could check in and we could have met for a dinner or dessert, or we could have planned a drink at home.

7. End with an expression of love.

Example 2:

Partner 1: I feel disregarded and unimportant when you do not discuss large purchases with me. I worry about our budget. (Or: It reminds me of when my dad would over–spend and we would have to eat canned beans for dinner.)

Partner 2: I heard you say: you feel trivialized and minimized when I do not talk to you when I buy big ticket items. You want to know our future is secure.

**Check in that Partner 1 feels understood. And Partner 2 understands. If so, move on, if not, start at the top.

How we will do better next time: We should have a limit for surprise gifts, and a budget for everything.

Expressions of love: I love you and I love how much you want to buy me tokens of love. I love you and I love how much you want to ensure our future.

Your turn. Do this together, taking turns. Think of a recent argument. Each of you will have an opportunity to be a speaker, and an active listener.

Partner 1:

"I feel…" Use three adjectives.

About

Insight/History

<u>Pause</u>: Does your partner understand you? Give them a chance to repeat back to you what you said <u>in their own words</u>.

Partner 2:

"What I heard you say is…" (This is your chance to confirm what you have understood.)

Do both of you feel heard and understood?

If not, start over. If so, move forward.

Together, decide: How will you do it better next time?

Both: End with an expression of love.

Your Partner's Turn:

Partner 2: "I feel…" Use three adjectives.

About

Insight/History

Pause: Does your partner understand you? Give them a chance to repeat back to you what you said <u>in their own words</u>.

Partner 1: "What I heard you say is… "

Do both of you feel heard and understood?

If not, start over. If so, move forward.

Together: How will you do it better next time?

Both: End with an expression of love.

Triggers

Minor situations can turn into major ones when triggers present themselves. Sometimes a minor thing can set us off. What causes this? It can be fatigue, hunger, frustration, or...a trigger.

Triggers are emotional sparks that sharply remind us of a previous, oftentimes traumatic event. In this case, we are speaking of triggers that negatively affect us. Suddenly, we are upset and we may not know why. Take a moment to breathe, acknowledge the feelings and talk through them. If you need assistance, please reach out to a professional, or to Mollie at Mollie@MollieSingh.com.

To learn more about triggers, please check out the following articles:

Psychology Today has a blog entitled: How to Spot Your Emotional Triggers:

https://www.psychologytoday.com/us/blog/the-gen-y-psy/201810/how-spot-your-emotional-triggers

When it is a trigger, it transports us to the past. If it is an especially emotional trigger, you can get flooded. It is absolutely imperative to take at least a 30-minute break in these situations.

We recommend at least 30 minutes because it takes a bit longer to come back to the present when triggered. It is then equally important to take time to come back to your loved one, and to acknowledge and discuss why you were triggered and what you think triggered you.

Remember you're on the same team, and you want to work through the triggering to strengthen your relationship. Furthermore, you want to process your trauma and the conflict to strengthen your relationship.

Hot Hint! If you find that your conflicts are often caused or exacerbated by triggers from past trauma, please contact Mollie or seek help from another Gottmann leader or your mental health professional to learn how to identify and de–escalate your reactions to triggers.

Owning Your Actions

When you do something right, you want to shout it from the rooftops, but what about when something goes awry?

Even when you had the best of intentions, things can go wrong. Do you own your responsibility for it? We suggest that there is ownership in everything you and your partner do. Wait...I own some of my partner's success?? Woohoo! But I own all their actions? Why?? Well, you are a partnership. That means you win together – and learn together. You are there to support each other, through thick and thin, through financial wins and losses.

Note: A word on getting mad, apologizing, and forgiving. Mollie's mamma would say, "Don't get so mad that you end up apologizing." This is sage advice. You should ask for a timeout if you feel out of sorts. However, Mollie would also add that it is really powerful to hear an apology. So, she apologizes often. We are all fallible. And, often, an apology is more of an acknowledgement that she hurt her love's feelings – even if it was unintentional.

Hot Hint! It is better to reach for progress, understanding, and love over perfection. Apologizing empowers progress. It promotes growth in yourself as well as your relationship. So, when one person comes back to apologize, accept it. Don't pile on. Let it go. If something nags at you, remember that salt pill. Let the situation deflate, then talk about it calmly. No fight is do or die. You're in this together.

A Note About "I'm sorry"

We often like to say, "I'm sorry, but..." and then launch into our reasoning. However, the qualification and explanation often leaves your partner feeling like they never really got an apology. So, instead, say, "I'm sorry, and" (find a way to validate your partner's feelings).

138

Rest assured, you will get your chance to receive the benefit when it is your turn to explain your side. For example, "I'm sorry I didn't mean to hurt you," is better than "I am sorry, but I was tired."

Win and Learn

At the end of the day, it does not matter what you or your partner say...what matters is how you make each other feel. Besides, words are often misunderstood and memories are fallible. And your disagreement is not a zero–sum game.

When you disagree, do not use absolutes – ever. And yes, we realize that is an absolute. That instance aside, when you are in conflict, words like 'never' and 'always' only serve to make your partner feel defensive and put them on their back foot with little room to recover. And in the end, how you recover from conflict is more important than the conflict itself. It offers the win that you both need in the moment to feel good.

There is no losing when it comes to conflict. You are both on the same team. You win together. And rather than losing, you learn together. One of the gifts of conflict is that while it starts with a disconnect, it leads to a better understanding of each other, which fosters growth and a deeper connection.

Chapter 11 Exercises

Exercise 1

Two Loves and a Wish

Think of a wish you had in the past and try this new technique.

Reflect: How was this different than the last time you experienced this issue?

Now, share your thoughts with each other. Make your plan to do it differently.

Exercise 2

Recall a minor disagreement:

Ask what is wrong.

Acknowledge the issue.

Ask for what you need – or ask how you can help.

Exercise 3

Discuss together

Each of you:

- Name a time you blamed your partner for a financial decision when you actually may have had some responsibility.

- Now share this with your partner. Yes, you are retroactively taking responsibility.

- Share how it feels when you do so.

- How did it feel to hear your partner take responsibility?

Recall the Law of Attraction: instead of looking for the mistakes your partner is making, try catching them doing something you can appreciate. Look for the positives, more will follow.

Exercise 4

Recall an argument where one person said "I'm sorry, but..."

Would the outcome change with the "I'm sorry, and..." approach? How?

Discuss with your partner. How would the outcome change?

For fun, let's take a light–hearted look at ourselves:

Answer the following for yourself and share with your partner.

I usually get cranky when_____ (for example: I am tired or hungry).

A rule of thumb when I am cranky is to_____ (for example: offer me coffee or a snack).

Sometimes, I just need_____ (for example, a shoulder to lean on, to be heard, a hug, to be quiet, to zone out).

A rule of thumb when I need_____ is to _____ (for example: A rule of thumb when I need a shoulder to lean on is to let me vent).

Note: While forecasting your emotions and needs can be a great exercise, this format can also be helpful in the moment. For example, if your love is trying to offer a solution that does not fit your needs, stop, appreciate the attempt, then ask for what you need.

Exercise 5

Plan ahead. Decide this together. When in conflict:

- Who leaves the room/premises? Remember not to linger in the same space after the timeout is called.

- How long will the timeout be?

- What will you do? Remember not to stew or think of rebuttals.

- When you come back, how will you return with love? We suggest sitting face to face, holding each others' hands and speaking to each other gently. Perhaps start with your Triple A's or Two Loves and a Wish.

If there is no plan to change, there will be no change.

Hot Hint! Please remember: When you take your break, it should be solo. Come back to each other in 20–30 minutes with a renewed sense of peace and a resolution to understand or solve the issue. And remember to always come back to complete the conversation.

Key points from Chapter 11:

- Timeouts are good. Decide when to come back. Each person gets a turn to discuss their perception of the event and their feelings around the event.
  - Stop and listen. Don't formulate your response without absorbing and understanding what your partner says.
  - Give one person a chance to express themselves. The other person should – in their own words – express what they heard. This allows each person to feel heard and understood.
  - If the partner is not fully understood, both parties should try again until each person feels like they are understood and that they understand the other's feelings.
  - Remember to hold hands. It changes the energy in the room.
  - Once both sides have had a chance to share their feelings, apologize – and mean it. Recall the salt pill – to have a conflict, two people are involved. Both parties play a role. Remember to use "I'm sorry, and..."
  - Come to an agreement on how to improve. This is your chance to express your needs and desires.
  - Express love to one another. Often.

- Please remember – Not even the gypsy's "magical" pill made everything perfect. You have the power to intentionally create the love affair of your wildest dreams with your partner. One experience at a time.

CHAPTER 12:
WHAT'S A CREDIT SCORE?

Do you know what a credit score is or how to improve it?

Back to our parable.

"So, tell me again, why do I have to use my earnings on the sale of my house to pay off the car and why you are the only one on the house loan?" he asked quizzically.

It was one of our early money conversations, and therefore was still civil.

"First, I am not the only one on the house. I am the primary, because I have a good credit score. You are on the house too. I am considered the primary because of my credit rating. We are buying this house together. You are paying off your truck because the interest rate is too high. And paying it off will help take one bill off of our plate, it will lower the total cost of the truck, and most importantly, it will improve your credit rating."

All of this made sense to me. It was like second nature to understand that good credit leads to better interest rates on loans. As The Splurger Type, he enjoyed his snowmobiles, his boat, his weekend home, and all of his other toys. As The Saver Type/Investor Type, I put more consideration into the resale of the condo I purchased and my future savings and purchasing power. Perhaps, had I been aware of and considered these differences, we would have had a better relationship.

Clients come to Joel all the time asking how they can improve their credit score. First, let's define what a credit score is. A credit score, also known as your FICO score (after the reporting agency, Fair Isaac Corporation) is used as a measure of your ability to borrow money. It also determines the interest rate at which you can borrow.

How is your FICO score calculated?

Sadly, that is a secret. No, we are not joking. We don't know exactly how it is calculated, but we do know, based on the information that is asked, what items are important.

These are the five most important factors in your credit score:

1. Your payment history. What does this mean? It is just shorthand for your timeliness of past credit payments. This accounts for 35 percent of your total FICO score and is the largest proportion of the overall score. The more late payments you have on your credit report, the lower your score will be. The goal is to pay on time as much as possible. Recall the couple in the parable. The husband had terrible credit, and the car loan was originally intended for him to demonstrate a history of paying his bills – no matter how exorbitant the interest rate. This was a chance for him to create a better payment history.

2. Outstanding debt. What is this? It is the amount you already owe on your credit card bills, mortgage or student loans. Obviously, the lower the amount the better, but ratios are important too (See below). This accounts for 30 percent of your FICO score. Again, recall the couple in the parable. Paying off the car loan would remove one item off the husband's credit list. This would eventually help with his credit rating.

3. Length of credit history. This represents 15 percent. So, if you are twenty–one, you are clearly going to have a much shorter credit history than someone who is in their 40s or 50s. The longer the history the better. Again, in the case of the couple in our story, we can see that the husband's history of not paying his debts was one of the factors that led to his poor credit rating.

4. Accounts in use (also known as your "credit mix"). The more accounts you have in use, the worse your credit score, in gen-

eral. The presence of many accounts will negatively impact your score whether you are using them or not! It also depends on what types of accounts are outstanding. If you have a home equity loan outstanding, this is viewed more favorably because there is collateral behind it—your home! Your credit mix accounts for 10 percent of the total FICO credit score.

5. Inquiries and new accounts. If you open multiple new accounts in a short period of time, this will negatively impact your credit score. Whenever a third party asks for your credit report (an "inquiry") this is recorded and if there are many inquiries in a short period of time, this will also negatively impact your score. Inquiries and new accounts (credit accounts) make up 10 percent of your score.

How many credit cards do you have, individually and as a couple?

Do you have joint cards?

And can you benefit from credit?

First of all, Joel has been an investor in Discover Financial Services (DFS), the company that owns Discover Card, on and off since he worked at Citigroup in 2010.

As an investor, does Joel care if you have ten cards or one? Well, Joel does, because he wants you to use your Discover card as much as possible. This is because DFS earns a fee—a transaction fee—every time you use the card.

Does Joel care if you pay your bill on time or not?

He doesn't, as long as you pay your bill at some point. See, if you pay your bill late, you incur late fees and interest expenses, so DFS—and Joel, as a shareholder—makes more money = more income for Joel.

Does Joel care if you don't pay your bill? Yes!

If you don't ever pay your bill, the company doesn't get any money from you, nor does Joel. This is called a "charge–off." And if you never pay your bill, then DFS doesn't ever get paid—that is not good for the company or Joel.

You should apply for more credit than you need especially on joint credit cards, so that you have capacity. For example, if you expect to be charging $1,000 a month, we recommend asking for a credit limit of at least $3,000. This allows for unexpected items—like an emergency car issue or if you need to travel unexpectedly. It also helps your credit score because of credit usage (see below). Remember, the FICO score is also based on availability of credit compared to net income.

How can you improve your credit score?

1. One way is to reduce your amount of credit outstanding. The quicker and sooner you can pay off any credit cards the better. Recall the couple: while credit card bills were not a point of contention between the two, the smaller balances were paid off, and paying off the truck helped to improve his credit score. Joel worked with one client who had more than $20,000 in credit card debt outstanding and was paying over $1,000 a month. Though that seems like a lot of money, he actually wasn't paying down his balances. It's important to understand: if you are only paying the minimum balance, you will not actually ever pay down your credit card.

   Thus, he opened a new account to transfer the balances onto a 0 percent interest rate card that was good for two years. This allowed him to come up with the cash in two years instead of right away, while not paying the average 11 percent interest rate which was causing the $1,000 a month payment. It's important to understand, while opening a new credit card caused a "hit" on his credit rating, it was temporary. Further, paying off the amount outstanding certainly helped his overall credit rating.

2. Lower the amount of your used credit limit. It might seem logical to just close out the credit card account you are not using. However, this impacts your use of credit. How much of your credit limit you use, will significantly impact your credit score If you are using 20 percent or less of your credit limits, this is a small percentage and will positively impact your credit score. Going to 40 or 50 percent of your allowable credit limit will weaken your FICO score, and if it is much higher than that, the score will be very depressed.

For example, say you had five credit cards each with a $10,000 credit limit and you were using four cards for an average of $2,500 a month, or $10,000 in total. Your utilization rate would be $10,000/$50,000 or 20 percent, but suppose you shut down the fifth card. Though the average amount was $2,500, you had only used this card for $500. Thus, the other cards had a total of $9,500. Now the utilization rate just jumped to $9,500/$40,000, or 24 percent. This would negatively impact your credit score.

Should I close a credit card account when I pay it off?

Consider simply leaving the credit card that you just paid off outstanding, and now your utilization rate actually goes down to 19 percent ($9,500/$50,000) from 20 percent ($10,000/$50,000).

3. Pay your bills on time. You can improve your credit score by paying on time. If you have five cards, over twelve months, you have sixty payments. Being on time for just two years in a row will greatly improve your credit score. Setting up an automatic deduction out of your checking or money market account will ensure that the balance is paid each month. And if you have spare cash at the end of the month, consider making an extra payment to one of your cards (assuming you don't pay your outstanding balance in full each month).

4. Stop applying for new credit cards. This includes gas and store cards. The more cards you apply for—especially within a three-month period—the lower your credit score will be. This is because each new credit card company does an inquiry as part of their background check, by looking at your credit report.

5. If possible, diversify your credit accounts. As we discussed earlier, having multiple types of credit accounts will help your score. For example, having a student loan, mortgage loan, and a credit card is better for your score than having just three credit cards—even if the amounts of the loans are the same or similar.

6. Finally, if you are ever rejected for any type of loan, get an explanation why. The credit card company should give you a specific explanation. For example, "you don't have a long enough credit history," or "you don't earn enough money," or "you are self-employed." Creditors prefer lenders whose compensation is consistent rather than volatile, like most entrepreneurs. If nothing else, they may find something on your credit report that you were unaware of. For example, years ago, when Mollie was trying to buy a house, her pre-qualification process showed an error on her credit history. She was able to correct it and have her credit return to her high score. This was an important lesson in monitoring her credit and ensuring her standing. What do you do to ensure your credit score improves or stays high?

One final comment on credit scores and credit usage.

Are you self-employed, an entrepreneur? If you are, then your income likely varies widely from month to month, and year to year.

The credit card companies don't love entrepreneurs because they like to see consistency. They don't like income that varies—even if it is growing significantly from year to year.

Joel's income has ranged from less than $60,000 to more than seven figures in the last ten years. Credit card companies don't like that, despite his earnings potential being much, much higher than any employee could take home. They still prefer someone at a "steady" job even if that person is earning $50,000 a year, year in and year out. If that's you, then know that your credit score is starting out at a higher level than someone who is an entrepreneur.

You can get your credit score for free if you are an American Express, Bank of America, or Discover cardholder. And, for full disclosure, many other banks and credit cards will also provide your credit score if you ask. They give it to you every month. Or you can get a free credit report annually from www.annualcreditreport.com. You can obtain your credit score as well as your report at www.myfico.com. Remember, FICO stands for Fair Isaac Corporation, the company that actually does the credit scoring.

Hot Hint! Your credit score will *not* go down if you request your credit score from any of the credit rating bureaus or even your credit card company.

What about LifeLock?

LifeLock is a paid service that protects your identity and your credit. They monitor the use of your personal information. You can even set up alerts for new accounts, spending limits and credit score changes. It does offer a guarantee should something go wrong. Mollie uses it and enjoys the feeling of security it offers.

Key Points from Chapter 12:

- Remember the five most important factors in your credit score: (1) your payment history; (2) outstanding debt; (3) length of credit history; (4) accounts in use; and (5) inquiries and new accounts.

- Find out your credit score and monitor it regularly

CHAPTER 13:
YOUR KID'S MONEY

Do you have children? If so, you are implicitly and explicitly teaching them about money. If you don't have children, feel free to skip this chapter. However, if you plan to have children, please read it. We believe it will provide some great fodder for your future.

Why is talking about your kids and money important? Well, you are shaping their future in every way. You send them to school, likely offer them extra–curricular activities, and play dates. You socialize them in every way. All of these things take some amount of money – even if it is a public school. Obviously, money is a necessary part of life. As such, financial education is also necessary. Financial experiences start at home. This chapter will help you with your kids and money.

Educating your children by having these conversations is the most important thing you can do. Money is a critical subject matter for you as an individual, you as a couple, and you as a family. We are not suggesting that you share all of the nitty gritty details of every account with your children, but rather that you consider introducing the topic of money to them early.

Why be open with the kids? Well, believe it or not, many kids grow up with wildly disparate ideas of their family's financial status and what it takes to live the life they are living. For example, many middle–class kids either think they are wealthy beyond their means, or that they have no money at all. If you educate your kids solely by the financial habits of their parents, or their money mindset, i.e., poverty versus abundant mindset, it can lead to huge issues in the children's financial expectations, and later habits.

Demonstrating a lifestyle that is aligned with your reality, as well as keeping an abundant mindset, is key. We are not saying to keep their thoughts revolving around money. Rather, we are suggesting that you inform and educate your children. The sooner they are comfortable with a financial understanding, the more responsible they are likely to be with their own money when they are grown up. If you are open, you can teach your kids how to appropriately manage financial issues and how to grow and maintain wealth. We want you and your children to have a prosperous mindset, even if or when money is tight.

Consider Joel's story: He started working early. His first job was delivering Pennysavers around Massapequa, Long Island, New York, and earning about a 1–2c per house that he supplied these advertisements to. For about 100 houses, he earned US$1–2 in 1976, which is about $18 for about an hour worth of work in today's (2021) U.S. dollars. His next job, at 14, was being a Little League Umpire. That was a big step up. For a 1.5–2 hour game, he earned about $5, which is worth about $40 in 2021. He then started working at Nathan's Famous Restaurant at the Sunrise Mall in Massapequa. He was just 16 and was earning a whopping $3.25 an hour. He remembers being so excited when the minimum wage was increased to $3.40 (a 4.6% raise for not doing anything!).

Joel kept on asking his boss to work more hours, but there were limits that a kid in the tenth grade with a full–time school schedule could work, especially, if he wanted to do his homework and get good grades. But the summers were different. He could work more! And then there was twelfth grade, when he could work even more, because his coursework during the second half of the year was considerably lighter.

Joel worked all those hours and saved so much because he had a defined goal: to get into a private university. He always knew he wanted to go to a private university and his dad had made a deal with him: If he could save up the money for the tuition for one year, then he could indeed go to his dream school. So, Joel did everything he could to save that money. And he did!

Did he have an allowance growing up? No.

Was that the right choice? Only you two, as parents, can decide that. Mollie also did not have an allowance growing up. She was performing paid dance performances as early as 11, and started working

155

when she was 14, two afternoons a week. As she got older, she took on more hours.

What does an allowance mean to you as a parent? Parents often wonder if they should give their children an allowance, especially when they are less than 10 years old and too young to work for others, perhaps.

First of all, we agree with Deborah L. Price, the author of *The Heart of Money*, with regards to allowances. Children should do something for the allowance, not just get paid $5 or $10 or $20 a week. Starting at a young age, children can do "chores" around the house including cleaning their room, putting dishes away after eating, or helping their parent's dry dishes after they are cleaned. They can take out the garbage or walk the dog. What about cleaning out the fish or frog's water–tank?

On the other hand, Mollie grew up with parents who believed that chores are a part of being in a family and sharing the living space. But she envied the freedom her friends had. One friend's parents gave this advice: Just as they had a day job, the kids' day job was to go to school. Just as they received feedback, and bonuses or pay raises based on that feedback, so did the kids. Mollie's parents did not take this advice though. So, when she started working at 14, it finally gave her the freedom she was craving. With that came the ability to pay some of her own bills – like her gas money and car insurance when that time came. Which approach is right for you? Take a moment to discuss and decide.

Ask each other:

1. Did you get an allowance as a kid?

2. How did it make you feel then?

3. In retrospect, what do you think of your parents' decision?

4. Do we want to give an allowance to the kids? Why or why not?

We believe that when children do some "work" for their pay they feel accountable for the job they do and it also builds self–esteem. It also teaches the value of money. Not just for the sake of money, but also for the time value of money; that the work they do gives them the commerce with which to purchase products and/or services for themselves.

Going back to Joel's story, he had a goal: to get into the private university. So, he saved and saved and saved some more. As we discussed earlier, being only an Accumulator Type can be detrimental to your money energy.

For Joel, he achieved his goal, but it really didn't teach him great money lessons.

Joel recommends teaching children the value of money early by establishing a checking and/or saving account before they are 10. Then, they can deposit money they get for birthdays or other occasions and see the balance in those accounts grow.

In *The 9 Money Rules Millionaires Use: Only The Unconventional Ones*, Joel establishes Rule #6 as Giving. It is a great lesson to teach children.

Joel recently had a conversation with his then 14–year–old daughter, Morgan, which went like this:

Joel: So, are you working for your mother this summer, Morgan?

Morgan: Yes.

Joel: What does she have you doing?

Morgan: Filing or doing research online.

Joel: How much do you plan to give to charities?

Morgan: What?

Joel: Morgan, you do remember Rule #6 (she read the book!).

Morgan: No, not really. What is that?

Joel: I recommend giving a portion of each dollar you earn to charities. Pick your favorite one and start small. In my book, I quoted John Templeton, one of the best money managers of all time, who said "I don't know anyone who has given at least 10% of his earnings each year over 10 years to charities who didn't have significantly more money at the end of the 10 years than at the beginning!"

Morgan: I'm just a kid!

Joel: It's not too early to start now!

Morgan: So, you do this?

Joel: Yes, of course. I started small—with less than 5% of my earnings, years ago—and now have committed to 10% each year.

Morgan: Really. What charities do you give to?

Joel: Well, my main one is the Food Bank of New York City which gives food to the homeless.

Morgan: That sounds like one I would like to give to.

Joel; Well, you should give to one that really resonates with you. Which one does right now?

Morgan: For me, right now, it would be some charity related to #BlackLivesMatter.

Joel: That is awesome. Start with the next check you get.

Lots of money issues in couples' relationships come from differences with dealing with children and money.

Teaching your children about money happens in big and small ways: It happens in the decision of an allowance; the activities we choose for them; it happens in the store when they want candy instead of fruit; it happens when they see a toy they want, but it's not in the budget. What you teach them about money is just as important in how you teach them. In other words, the words you use are high-ly influential. So, instead of saying: "that's too expensive. We can't afford that!" Why not say: "That is not a priority for us right now!" And if you choose to say something like, "I will think about it." Please remember to come back and talk to them about why or why not they are getting that treat or toy. Saying "I will think about it," is a great way to put some time between you and the impulse.

Hot Hint! Compulsions, like anger, pass given a good thirty min-utes. By circling back and having the conversation with your kids, you demonstrate the skill of reasoning and follow–through that you want to instill in them. It also offers the great lesson of delayed gratifica-tion. Lastly, it fosters communication.

Consider a recent experience between Joel and his then 16–year–old daughter, Lauren, in Newport, Rhode Island. She wanted a $55 sweatshirt which looked really great on her. To Joel, it didn't seem worth the price.

There are plenty of sweatshirts you can get for $20 or $25, but she really wanted this one.

In this scenario, which is played out daily across the world by par-ents and children, what is the best course of action?

If the child is too young to be working and you have decided not to give allowances, then one option is to just say "this is not a priority for us right now." Spending that $55 on 3–4 days of groceries for the family is a higher priority.

Many experts suggest visual cues for younger children. Consider using a clear jar, rather than a decorative piggy bank. This way they can see what they have. Or a bar chart on the wall. And when they want something, they can see how much comes out of their account.

If your child is getting an allowance, let them make the decision. "Would you like to use the next 3 weeks' worth of allowance to buy that yourself?" This is a great way to teach consequences.

If your child is older and working, then they can use their own money to buy it: "If it is a priority for you, then use your money to get it."

An alternative to that is to contribute to the sweatshirt by saying, "$55 seems a bit high for the value but if you really want this one instead of the ones that go for $20, I will contribute $20 and you can pay the rest." Another option here is to teach the value of time and money. Perhaps put off the purchase until they can make the money for it. Maybe let them have a lemonade stand until they can earn the money for the desired item.

Mollie had a neighbor whose children would move the garbage cans to and from the street on trash days for $15 per month. They were quite young, so they only worked on Mollie's street. But they would leave an invoice in her mailbox every month and managed to do this for 5 neighbors. One of the kids chose to save all his money, while the other spent it the minute he got it. Both learned valuable lessons in the process.

Another common question is: "should I tell my children about my monetary situation if it is not positive? For example, our cash flow is negative and we can't afford to go on vacation this year."

We recommend being open and honest with your children. Children are very astute, and they can tell what the real situation is, even if you are not telling them. Now, the type of discussion, will be completely different depending on your child's age.

For the younger children—between four and 10, we recommend explaining to them what is going on in simple terms: "Because of my recent job loss, there will be less money to spend on things. Everyone will work together to cut back a little bit." You can explain that certain expenses will be eliminated until the money starts flowing again. Then, you and your spouse can decide which costs can be cut (some to think about: cable, video games, Apps that have monthly subscription fees, private lessons, summer camps, vacations).

For the older children (over 10 years old), you can go into more detail about the amount of money the job you lost had been producing and how much you have in your emergency account and savings which could be used for monthly expenditures.

Remember to consider both, your and your spouse's money personality type. Also, please consider your and your spouse's history in finances and setbacks when dealing with children — whether it is about spending on a whim, the loss of a job, or the day–to–day financial decisions. The varying money types will definitely have an impact on how you deal with your children in every situation. One of you may feel it is okay to spoil a child by giving them everything they want, while the other believes in teaching them about saving and giving.

We recommend having this discussion before you have children, but if you are reading this and already have them, the present is the best time! Stop reading! Close the book and have the discussion on how to approach savings and giving with your children...right now!

Two more common questions, Joel gets are:

Should we save for college when we can barely save for retirement?

And, my children, are 14 and 16, is it too late to save for college?

Let's answer the 2nd one first: it's definitely not too late. For the 14–year–old, there are 4 years until they start college and another 3 before they start their senior year of college. In 7 years, if you are saving $5,000 a year, you could actually fund almost 2 years of tuition based on the average out–of–state public college. And even if you are thinking about a private college, that would be sufficient for about 1.5 years of those colleges. Another option for your kids would be community college for the first two years. It is an economical option. And many have direct relationships with local 4 years colleges. They will give you the exact educational path to succeed.

For the 16–year–old, there are still 2 years until they start college and another 3 before they start their senior year of college. In 5 years, if you are saving $5,000 a year, you could actually fund about a year and a half of the average out–of–state public college and about one year of a private college's average tuition.

Joel's recommendation for the other question is: retirement not college savings. You can take a loan out for their college education, or your children can. And that loan, by the way, can be relatively inexpensive compared to other kinds, like a personal loan.

Most borrowing rates for student loans are much lower than the going rate for a credit card or a personal loan, and even similar to a mortgage loan which, by the way, is collateralized by the real estate you purchased. For the 2020–2021 school year, the federal student loan interest rate for undergraduates is 2.75% (!). Federal rates for parent loans are higher—5.3%. The average 30–year mortgage loan rate in late–2020 was 3% and home equity loans 4.5 percent. The average credit card rate was 23% and personal loans ranged from 5–20% depending on your credit score.

An alternative to doing all or nothing is if you are contributing 10% of your pre–tax earnings to a retirement fund, you can reduce your contribution for the years you want to contribute to a college savings fund. One recommendation would be to reduce your retirement contribution for a few years to 6% and put the other 4% of pre–tax earnings to the college fund. You can always engage your child in saving for their own university education as Joel's father did with him.

Chapter 13 Exercises

Exercise 1

Answer these questions separately and then come back together to discuss them:

1. How much money is the "appropriate" amount to give our children when they are 6 years old? 10? 12? 14? 16? 18?

2. Is it ok to fight about money in front of the children? Does it matter what age they are? For example, yes, at 16, but no at 4?

3. If one of our children is angry at us, is it ok to give them $10 or $20 to placate them, so they are less angry?

4. Is it ok for our children to ask me for money when you say "no" and me to give it to them (or vice–versa)? If it is not ok, take a moment now to discuss your plan of action when a child asks for money.

5. If I'm spending two weeks straight working late at the office or if I have missed their play, is it ok to come home and give the children big gifts?

Key Points from Chapter 13:

- Children should do something for their allowance, not just get paid $5 or $10 or $20 a week.

- Start teaching your kids at a young age about money and money consequences.

- Find gentle and encouraging ways to discuss money with your kids.

- Be open and honest with your children. They are very astute and can tell what the real situation is, even if you are not telling them.

- If you must choose between contributing to your retirement fund and saving for your kid's college education, contribute to your retirement fund, but remember one alternative is to cut your contribution and provide some money to your children's college fund.

CHAPTER 14:
SHOULD WE USE CREDIT?

We return to our parable:

"So, what is the deal with the $19,000?" The arbitrator asked as he came bursting into the room.

"What $19,000?" My attorney and I asked in unison.

"Well," he sunk into his seat and leaned forward interested, "he mentioned something about paying off your dad's truck or something being your dad's fault, I honestly couldn't understand him. He was yelling, though, he was clear that he wanted his money back."

My attorney started combing through the big notebook of accounts I had compiled for her. Then she looked over at me accusingly.

"What? No! My dad never had a truck," I sighed deeply and continued, "my ex-husband had a truck. It was worth about $7,000. Maybe less... Anyway, because of his bad credit and high interest rates, he owed over $21,000. But the pay–off was $19,000. And since his house had sold, and we were trying to get his credit score up, we paid it off."

"So, why did he say it was your dad's fault?"

"Well, I talked to my dad about finances all the time. When I ran the numbers, it did not make sense to me, so I called my dad." He was always trying to coach me about interest rates and credit.

"So, it was his truck, and his loan? And you saved him money and it improved his credit rating?" The mediator asked.

So, is credit good or bad?

Well, it depends. What are you using it for?

In our parable, credit was bad. The interest rate being paid was high and it was a depreciating asset (the car's value goes down every year).

But is using credit always bad? Of course not! Had he had a low interest rate loan on the car – say less than 2%, then the couple could have earned more interest in an investment and it would have been beneficial to have a loan.

Credit is obviously based on trust. In the story above, it clearly shows that the bank did not trust him with a car loan. How can we see that? Well, the interest rate was extraordinarily high. He had a 19.6% interest rate – almost as much as the average credit card.

A little more background – his personal credit rating was so bad, but he needed a new car, so they gave him this loan. Had he shown he could be trusted to pay his bills in a timely manner, his interest rate would likely have been much lower. So, why did they give him a loan? Because he convinced them that he could and would pay them back. So, the higher interest rate and longer loan period insured they would at least get paid for the vehicle. But, also, if he paid the loan in its entirety, they would get paid many times over (because of the interest rate).

As the picture at Moody's Investors Service in downtown Manhattan states below: "Credit is based on "Man's Confidence in Man."

So, again, is credit good or bad?

It depends. It hinges on what you borrow for. In the above example, if the car was an absolute necessity to get to work, then sure it was a good idea. If however, it was a recreational vehicle that may put constraints on your finances, then no. It was not a good credit option, especially because cars are a depreciating asset.

And to be honest, it is a trick question. Why? Because without the background, you wouldn't have known the interest rate on his car loan. But given his interest rate – and that it is a depreciating asset, credit was a bad idea. The only reason to take it was absolute need and a way to rebuild his credit rating – if he had chosen to make payments in a timely manner.

Conversely, if he had great credit, and the interest rate was lower than 3%, then he could make a higher return investing the bulk of his money elsewhere and credit would be a great thing.

Another use of credit is in your stock account. We know some sophisticated investors who took advantage of some very inexpensive stock prices in 2009. In most securities accounts, you can borrow from the brokerage company. You do have to fill out a form to establish a "margin account," which is just a fancy term for an account which is on credit. Anyway, these investors borrowed from their brokerage account at 5–10 percent interest rates and invested in securities that proceeded to go up 50–100 percent over the next year or two. What a great use of credit!

According to David Graeber, in his International best seller, *Debt: The First 5,000 Years*, Calvin, alive in the 1500s, was one of the first to argue that charging interest on a loan was reasonable. "And by 1650 almost all Protestant denominations had come to agree with his position that a 'reasonable' rate of interest (usually 5 percent) was not sinful."

How was all this justified? First, Protestant thinkers all continued to make the old medieval argument about interest: "that 'interest' is really compensation for the money that the lender would have made had he been able to place his money in some more profitable investment." Graeber went on to explain that loans were 'legalized' in 1545, and being a lender became a real job for those who didn't have any other income source.

If one looks at the history of debt, there is a lot of confusion as to the morality of borrowing. In fact, Graeber explains that, in general, we humans believe two things about it: "(1) paying back money one has borrowed is a simple matter of morality, and (2) anyone in the habit of lending money is evil." So, how to do we borrow, if it is evil to lend?

Have you bought a house? Then you borrowed money — unless you paid for it all in cash!

Graeber goes on to state that: "It is almost impossible to find a single sympathetic representation of a moneylender . . . by definition one who charges interest." He goes on to explain that "The very word, 'usurer,' evokes images of loan sharks, blood money, pounds of flesh, the selling of souls, and behind them all, the Devil, often represented as himself a kind of usurer, an evil accountant (not an actuary!) . . . biding his time until he can repossess the soul of a villain who, by his very occupation, has clearly made a compact with Hell."

Chapter 14 Exercise

Exercise

Answer together:

- How do you and your partner feel about borrowing money?

- Have you and your partner borrowed from:

  ◦ A bank?

  ◦ A credit card company?

  ◦ Your mom or dad?

  ◦ A sibling?

- How does debt make you feel?

As you discuss these things, ask the following:

1. What is the story behind the answer?

2. How did it make you feel in the moment?

3. How does it make you feel now?

4. Ask any additional questions that come to mind. With love. No judgements here.

Key Points from Chapter 14:

- Credit is based on "Man's Confidence in Man!"

- Is credit good or bad? It depends! It hinges on how you are using it and what your return is on the credit you use.

CHAPTER 15:
WHERE IS YOUR CASH GOING?

We return to our parable:

> "But I make six figures!! You don't! Why do I have to be on a budget??," he yelled at me.

> "I am not your mother – I am not telling you what to do. We both decided on this budget," I sighed. "Also, you make $120,000 per year, gross. Not take home. You actually only bring home 60% after taxes. And you have debt and bills. And some of those bills are monthly expenses for your toys including insurance, moorage and storage fees," I said counting the boat, the snowmobiles, and the second house, and reminding myself of how completely different our opinions of money matters were.

> "And why did you make me pay off my truck? I earned that money on my house! I should be able to spend it on my stuff!" he shouted.

> "Made you pay off??? I didn't make you do anything. And you did spend it on your stuff! You owed that money on your truck. In fact, you owed way more money than the truck is actually worth. And we saved thousands of dollars paying it off early. Plus, the payoff will help your credit score," I said sighing deeply. I think this was the millionth time I explained this.

> "I'm going for a drive!" he screamed as he slammed the door shut. The house shook. And I sank into the couch relieved to be done with the shouting match.

> Within 30 minutes, there was a credit alert on our bank card. Someone was attempting to spend $7,000 on the card. After I finally got his credit cleaned up, we set up alerts for excessive spending. I tried calling and texting him to find out if this was him. I got no answer. So, I declined the charge secretly happy to have thwarted what I assumed was another one of his an-

gry spending moments. But he got even angrier. And when he came home, he was even more enraged.

"How could you???"

"What?" I asked wearily.

"I was trying to buy something!"

"Oh, so that was you?" I asked, as innocently as I could muster. "I tried to call and text you."

"Well, if I can't have my camera, we are not going to Los Angeles!" he yelled. I honestly think he had two notes – sweet and screaming. There was no in between.

"What, why?" I asked incredulous. "That is in the budget. And that is already paid for. And not with credit! If we cancel now, we will actually lose money."

"We always go to your family's place!"

"No. We budgeted to go four times a year. We actually always go to the country house," I countered, "a house we work for more than we should. A Bed and Breakfast that should be run as a business and generating income. But instead, it is used as a weekend retreat place. And I am the one who is always cleaning it." By now, I was tipping toward his side of angry. I couldn't handle it. Not only did we have a difference in opinion on how to share and spend money, we fundamentally had differences of opinion on how to spend our spare time. We were diametrically opposite when it came to planning our future. He planned for the weekend. I planned for the years ahead.

Before him, my typical weekend included getting chores done, meeting up with some friends for dinner or a movie, and even taking some time to educate. Sure, I loved to travel and play. But his play was usually my work. The country house usually needed some airing and cleaning out.

As I did these chores, my dad's voice echoed in my ear, "Work smarter, not harder, honey. Save. Educate. Invest." I used to do this. Now, I wasn't doing any of this. I wanted more out of life. He wanted more of his life to be play. In the end, I had no time for my kind of fun or the future.

Do you have the time to post on Facebook, Instagram and Snapchat every day?

Do you have time to watch sports this weekend or play golf with your buddies?

Or go shopping with your friends?

Do you have time to watch that movie or binge your favorite TV program?

If you answered "yes" to any of those questions and you are not budgeting, you do have the time. You are just not making it a priority!

We know couples who will spend a hundred and fifty hours planning for a five–hour event — their wedding. Yet, they won't spend fifty hours a year – equivalent to one hour a week for financial freedom planning. Isn't thirty years of your life (or more) worth fifty hours a year? That is not to say that the wedding isn't worth your time and effort. Indeed, it is a momentous occasion. That said, it is one occasion. What we are suggesting is spending some time to plan for the many years to come.

Let's Start With Your Budget

First, let's define it – what is a budget?

A budget is an estimate of expected income and expenses for a given period in the future. Having and adhering to a budget is Rule #7 in *The 9 Money Rules Millionaires Use: Only The Unconventional Ones*.

First, we will start with identifying what your current budget is –

what you actually spend on. Here are the steps:

1. Please check Appendix 4 for a sample spreadsheet. This will help you create and manage your budget. There will be different categories including food, shelter, chocolate, massages, manicure/pedicure, lottery, fantasy games (baseball, football, etc.), gas, etc., etc.

2. Keep track of every amount you spend for one day. Yes everything. If you bought that pack of gum, write it down. If you purchased a coffee or a water or a soda, write it down. Maybe you love having that piece of chocolate or M&Ms (peanut or plain?); write that down. Write it all down.

3. You will put the amounts in the appropriate cell in the spreadsheet.

4. You will fill in your monthly income as a couple. This should be your net income, after taxes and other automatic contributions for retirement savings like 401(k), 403(b), etc.

5. You will subtract #3 from #4 above to get your monthly net cash flow.

6. Is the total from step 5 positive? Congratulations. You are one of the single–digit percentage of couples who are not spending all they make. Is the result from step 5 negative? If yes, we have some work to do!

The next step is to determine how close or far away you are from financial freedom. After which, adjusting your budget will be key.

"Financial freedom is being able to spend time (as much as you want) with the ones you love." — Doug Nelson, Bestselling author of *Catch Fire: How to Ignite Your Own Economy*

Hot Hint! Your goal is to understand where your partner is coming from with their answers and where they want to go with your finances.

If you haven't filled out the Financial Freedom Survey – Appendix

5, please stop reading and fill out the whole survey:
https://www.salaurmor.com/prosperity-survey/

For Joel, financial freedom, as a concept, is doing what he loves, with whom he loves, for as much time as he loves to do it, and where he loves to do it.

For Mollie, financial freedom means learning new things, traveling, helping people, seeing shows, and meeting up with friends wherever and whenever.

You will notice that we are essentially saying the same thing. We just worded it differently.

Any way you choose to word your version is great. It offers your partner the insights as to what is important to you. As Mollie describes in her couples' workbook – *Infinitely Loving: A Workbook to Support Couples in Creating a Life of Love Together*, the way you define things is going to differ based on your experiences. Those experiences brought you together, and now it is time to build together.

The specific, calculated definition for financial freedom is to add up all your expenses for a month.

Example: Let's assume your expenses add to $5,000. You multiply that amount by 12 for 12 months. That equals $60,000. Assuming you earned 6% interest per year on your investments, you would need $1 million, to earn that $60,000. So, once you have $1 million then you would be financially free.

Monthly Expenses * 12 = Annual Expenses

Passive Income + (Investments * income earned on those investments) ≥ Annual Expenses

That $1 million must earn 6%. It can't be your house. Nor your retirement fund. Please note: We are not suggesting that you must save 100% of that million dollars. We are suggesting you invest your savings wisely and take advantage of compounding interest.

People ask Joel: "Why not, isn't that part of my assets?"

Joel's response is: "It's not earning any money *now*." And if you are 25 and you have to wait 40 years for that money, then you're not financially free now. The goal is to find your current financial freedom number. We want you to be financially free before you retire.

Let's expand on the 6%. You should expect your investments to earn 6% annually. It is fair to note that markets fluctuate. For example, at the low of the Covid19 pandemic's impact on the stock market (March 23, 2020), the S&P 500 had dropped 33%. This can be quite unsettling for many. However, historically, markets always rebound and grow. As of this writing (August 19, 2020) the stock market was up 51% from that. In fact, the stock market was at an all–time high – surpassing the previous all–time high from February 2020.

Hot Hint! The stock market is not a reflection of the current economy. When the economy is in a slump, you will hear about many people making money on stocks. Why is this? A stock's value is the present value of its future earnings. For example, Hershey's did so well during the Great Depression of the 1930s because despite the circumstances of the times, they continued to invest in their business and employees, thereby setting them up for success in the future.

Let's go back to your financial freedom number: You should include only the assets that are earning money for you now. If you rented out part of your house or you bought a second home, you're generating rental income! Or you have stocks that are paying dividends, or you're trading stocks and generating income from that. Or maybe you have a side business: An Amazon fulfillment business or any side business that is generating income today for your financial freedom. We define passive income below.

> Mollie: So, Joel, what if I am doing exactly what I love and getting paid for it?

> Joel: First, congratulations on doing exactly what you love and getting paid for it. And second, that is active income. Because you are actively working for it.

What are your highest priorities?

We now know what financial freedom means to you, but how do you prioritize your dreams and desires?

Great question!

Have the conversation with your partner. Take a moment and refer back to Chapter 2 and review how you each answered what financial freedom means to each of you.

Do you have a better understanding of what Financial Freedom means to your partner?

Does this help with your own understanding of what Financial Freedom means to you?

How do you both match up?

So, what exactly is passive income? It is the earnings and investments that are outside of your retirement accounts that generate income without you having to work for them. If you have your own coaching business, that income does not count as passive income. That is active income!

Passive income can include the income generated from:

- Stocks (i.e., the dividend income on those stocks)

- Rental real estate property

- An Amazon fulfillment business that you only work on 2–3 hours a week

- Bond income

- A book or books that you wrote

All that is passive income.

Now the question is: "How close are you to financial freedom?" The financial freedom survey Joel created (see Appendix 5) helps people to calculate what they need. However, most people guess. And when they do, they come up with really large numbers such as $5 million, $10 million, or $25 million. Then they calculate the actual number together. And everyone gets excited because, for most people, it's not much more than a million dollars.

Let's pause to discuss one million dollars. Does that number feel huge to you? Intimidating? It may seem that way at first glance. But consider this, there are plenty of ways to generate passive income.

There are many, many ways to generate a million dollars and plenty no one can enumerate.

Here are just a few:

- You invested in stocks and they generated income.

- You inherited some money. You invested it wisely and it is now growing at a dramatic rate.

- You paid yourself first (that is, you took money out of your paycheck every time you got paid and put it into an investment earning at least 8%. If you invested $1,000 a month for 25 years starting at 35, you would be a millionaire by 60).

For one particular couple, their financial freedom number was less than half a million dollars given where they lived and their expenses. They had already saved enough to generate $100,000 in passive income. And that's actually not far away from being financially free. And in just five or seven years they could be financially free! They got excited. "We are pretty close."

So, do the calculation with your partner. Tally up your total amount of passive income that you have together. Add up your current net worth – do the research if you do not know off the top of your head. Then calculate your financial freedom number.

Please take into consideration the lifestyle you want in the future. Like Mollie, when you retire, you may want to sell that house and move into an assisted living place or into an apartment.

Mollie: I will tell you that my husband and I recently made the decision to sell our large house. This is one of the best decisions we've ever made. The house was too big for our current needs and neither of us wanted to work for the house anymore. There was too much maintenance. Now we feel free and, we've generated income from that house. Also, we have completely cut down our expenses for maintenance.

Joel: Have the discussion! Your expenses may change. One thing in that equation is what are your expenses today? But those expenses, that $5,000, that we gave you in that example for one month, could go up or down when you move to that next stage of life. A lot of times, it is going to go down.

Don't forget to consider commuting expenses: you may not need a car. You may not need a house. You may want to move into an apartment. These expenses could actually go down, and then, believe it or not your financial freedom number goes down!

Mollie: Right! And moving to the new apartment allowed us to go down to being a one car household. Another expense removed! Of course, we may decide later to re-enter the housing market. And our financial freedom number has that possibility in consideration. But for now, this was the right decision for us.

Understanding your Net Worth

Let's start with your assets. Add up all your investments: stocks, bonds, mutual funds, your house, any vacation homes, rental real estate property, 401(k), 403(b), 457, annuities, Roth IRAs, traditional IRAs, cash value life insurance, and cash and short-term investments: checking, savings, money market, and CD accounts.

This is the amount of your total assets.

Now add up all your debt. This includes home equity loans, mortgage loans, credit card debt (only the amount that you don't pay off monthly), student loans, car loans, and anything else you owe.

Taking your total assets less your total debt is your net worth.

Subtract from your total assets any money you have in any retirement funds—those 401(k), 403(b), 457, Roth IRAs, traditional IRAs, and fixed and variable annuities. Also, your house, your cash–value life insurance, and cash and short–term investments earnings less than 2% (we could include them, but if this amount is less than $50,000, then the total annual income is less than $1,000). What is left over is the amount of your passive income investments.

You can see how close you are to financial freedom by subtracting your passive income investments from your financial freedom number. Remember, you calculated it by multiplying your monthly expenses by 12 and then dividing by 6%. If it is negative, then that means you are financially free already!

One important question people ask Joel when he discusses financial freedom is:

Why does my money in retirement accounts (like a 401(k) or a traditional and Roth IRA) not count toward my financial freedom number?

I'm closer to financial freedom when I contribute to a retirement account, aren't I?

Here is our reason why retirement accounts are not counted: If you are over 59.5, you have access to this money and can count it in your financial freedom number, but only if it is generating income for you through interest or dividends. Then, it is generating income for you now.

What we mean here is that if you have access to the earnings in your retirement accounts so that you can take the money out and use it today, then it can be included in your financial freedom number. So, if your stocks pay dividends and they are available to live off of or you have invested in bonds and the income from those bonds are available to live off of, then you can include those amounts towards your financial freedom number.

However, that is only true for a Roth IRA which you have already paid income taxes on. If you want to add in the money from a traditional IRA or 401(k) or 403(b), you should "tax affect" it by applying your tax rate (use 30 percent to be conservative) to the amount in it. For example, you have $100,000 in your 401(k) and you are over 59.5, then only $70,000 is available to you after taxes. Another important point is that you may not be generating any passive income if the account it is in does not pay dividends or is losing money.

For those of you who can't get access to this money without paying a 10 percent penalty on top of the tax rate, it is not included in your passive income because it is not generating any income for you now. If you want to retire early—before 65 (some of you want to retire a lot younger than 65), then excluding your retirement savings is appropriate since it is not going to generate any income for you until much later in life. If you are 25, 35, or 45, you must wait at least 15 years to get access to your retirement money without a penalty. That is why Joel recommends excluding your retirement funds in the financial freedom calculation. If you have further questions, email Joel at Joel@SaLaurMor.com.

Are you in debt?

Here is a method that Joel highly recommends using. It will allow your cash flow to improve fast. We call it "The Budget Game."

The main points of the method are from one of our favorite books, *Ask and It is Given*, by Esther and Jerry Hicks (https://www.salaurmor. com/inspiration/#books)

> To begin the process, grab a pen and paper or open up a spreadsheet. Start with the far–left column, write a heading that describes your largest expense (it is usually your rent or your mortgage payment), and on the next line under the header, write the dollar amount. Circle this amount, which is the sum you are obligated to pay each month. On the third line, write the total amount of the debt outstanding.

- Do the same for the second largest expense and the third, until you get to the smallest one.

- Across the top of all the columns write: "It is my desire to keep my promise regarding all these financial obligations, and in some cases, I will even do twice as much as required."

- Each time you receive a bill, get out your paper or spreadsheet and adjust, if necessary, the minimum monthly amount that is required.

- The first time you receive a bill or when it's time to make the payment for the category on the far—right column of your paper or spreadsheet (the smallest expense you have), write the check for exactly twice the amount that is required.

- Then, also write in the new amount of that outstanding balance.

- This may seem a little strange, but even if you don't have enough money to pay everything you owe in all the columns, be sure to double the payment in the far—right column.

- Now feel glad that you have kept your new promise to yourself to do your best to pay everything you owe, and to pay twice that amount in some cases. It is that glad feeling that will help you move forward with this exercise. The better you feel about this, the more you will want to feel better.

- You are looking at your finances in a new way: creating a new vibration! The new vibration will help you create a new circumstance. And as stated in the earlier point, when you add good feelings to a vibration, more of that will follow.

- If you will take the time to really enter everything you owe on the paper or in the spreadsheet, your newly focused attention will begin to positively activate circumstances around the subject of money for you. Because like attracts like. It is the Law of Attraction.

- Instead of feeling discouraged about getting bills in the mail, you will now feel an eagerness to enter the bill in your spreadsheet or on your paper.

- This shift in your attitude and vibration will create shifts in your financial picture. Money that you were not expecting will appear in your experience. Bargains will appear; your dollars will start going farther.

- Be consciously aware that these things are happening in response to your newly focused attention and the resultant shift in your vibration.

- As extra money appears, you will find yourself eager to apply another payment to the spreadsheet, and soon that debt will be repaid, and you can eliminate that column from your spreadsheet or on your paper.

Hot Hint! 'Vibration' is another way of describing the energy emanating from an object. Often, it is the energy you have assigned to it. So, if you do the budget game and start having good feelings toward your budget, then your finances will start to feel good. And the Law of Attraction tells us that we will attract even more good things when we feel good.

Column after column will disappear as your financial gap between what is coming in and what is going out widens. Your sense of financial well–being will also improve as you play. And if you will take the game seriously, your vibration around money will shift so significantly that you can be debt–free in a very short period of time!

One of Joel's clients played this game seriously and in just a few weeks she had multiple job offers (she was working part–time when she started the game). What happens when you play the game each day is that your point of attraction will shift from a focus on resistance (the debt) to a focus on allowance (the abundance and prosperity). And once you allow, you will feel freer and anything will be possible!

Let's be clear about our view on budgeting. Many have said budgeting is just focusing on lack, scarcity, and a poverty consciousness. To us, you need to know where you are, before you can figure out where you want to go. If you don't know how much money you are spending now — what your current expenses are — how can you figure out what it will take to become financially free, based either on your current or dream expenses?

Yes, some financial "gurus" will tell you to cut out those lattes at Starbucks and drive only used cars (please see the Ways to Save Chapter – Chapter 5), but that won't, in our humble opinion, get you to financial freedom, alone. If you can't increase your income and especially generate passive income to exceed your expenses, you won't ever become financially free.

We recommend:

If you truly want to become financially free, sit down with your partner and write down your dream expenses. That is the amount of expenses you would have if you were living your dream life. For example, do you want to take an annual vacation? Or do you want to spend the summers elsewhere?

Second, now get very specific about how you would live if you could live your dream life. The more specific the better. Instead of writing down that you would like to have a dream car worth at least $50,000, write down that you would like to own a blue convertible Maserati Quattroporte S with brown leather seats and a 424 HP V6 with intelligent RWD and semi–autonomous driving capabilities. And write what these things mean to each of you. Understand the "why" behind the desire. As you visualize the Maserati – or whatever car is your dream car – be sure to dwell in the feeling that car will give you. Then dream of it, or better. Let the Universe help you dream bigger.

Why be specific?

Because the more specific you can be with your dreams and desires, the more the subconscious mind will dwell on it, imagine it, and feel the feelings of driving it, with the top down and the wind blowing your hair. We encourage you to go one step further and tell yourself, "this or better." This helps you stay open to the possibility of greatness beyond your dreams.

We actually want to get you into the feeling of what these things offer you. Once you have the feeling, you will attract more of that feeling.

Also, importantly, to reaching your goals, it is helpful if you know what your specific goals are. And once you write down all your dream material items (remember – this or better), you can add up the costs of buying them outright or leasing them and see what the amount your financial freedom number would be.

Chapter 15 Exercises

Exercise 1

Ask each other the following:

- What does Financial Freedom mean to you?

- What are your highest priorities?

Exercise 2

Calculate and discuss your joint Financial Freedom Number with your partner.

What is your current net worth?

Your net worth is your assets less any amounts you owe. So, you could say:

NW (for net worth)=A (assets) – D (for debt)

Exercise 3

Discuss your feelings and beliefs about money.

How do you feel about $1 million dollars?

> Does it feel huge and intimidating? If so, why?

> Does it feel like it is not enough? If so, why?

What number feels achievable?

Do you think rich people can't be spiritual or good souls?

Or do you feel that this number is just too big to ever truly be accumulated?

Where does this belief come from?

Key Points from Chapter 15:

1. Calculate all of your assets! These include your investments: stocks, bonds, mutual funds, exchange–traded funds (ETFs), your house, any vacation homes, rental real estate property, 401(k), 403(b), 457, annuities, Roth IRAs, traditional IRAs, cash value life insurance, and cash and short–term investments: checking, savings, money market, and CD accounts.

- Add up all the liabilities—all your debt in the relationship. These include home equity loans, mortgage loans, credit card debt (only the amount that you don't pay off monthly), student loans, car loans, and payday loans, which we know some of you have.

- Calculate your net worth as your total assets less your total liabilities.

- Ask yourselves: are your total assets growing or shrinking?

- Is your net worth going up or down each year? You should be calculating it jointly at the beginning of January of each year for the prior year.

- What is your net cash flow? Is it positive or negative? This will give you a strong indication if you are moving closer to financial freedom or not.

- How much passive income do you have?

- What is your financial freedom number? How close are you to being financially free (hint: subtract from your financial freedom number your passive income investments)?

- How much credit are you using to support your lifestyle? The more credit outstanding, the more likely that you are farther from financial freedom. There are many good uses of credit, and if you can earn substantially more than what you are paying in credit, it probably makes sense to borrow. It is worthwhile to check into credit cards that offer cash back or other incentives.

2. Take the time to talk with each other. Discuss what Financial Freedom means to each of you. Consider each other's highest priorities. Please remember to ask open ended questions to understand where your partner is coming from with their answers and where they want to go with their finances.

3. Dream, then dream bigger. Write out your dream expenses. Get specific about why you want what you want. Feel the victory of obtaining it. Then dream about that great vacation – or better! Going first class….or in a private plane!

Concluding Letter

Dear Couple,

Thank you for investing in your relationship and taking this extraordinary journey with us. We know that life, love, and money can be challenging at times. We hope you found inspiration and helpful techniques and solutions to those challenges within these pages to support you on your journey to *Infinite Love and Money*.

We shared many ways to improve your relationship with money and with each other. We also covered how improving one of those relationships can feed the improvement of the other.

The exercises ask you to take action to improve your communication and your emotional response to difficult situations, as well as to resolve conflict and make important decisions together about money, savings, and investing. There is no need to incorporate all the lessons, exercises and actions at once. It takes time to develop new habits and methods. As such, we recommend you take your time. Start with one small change that you're excited about. Make a commitment to yourself, and to each other, to stick with it. Consider concentrating on this one change for 30 days. Then, when it feels comfortable, move to the next change. For more information on how to make changes, please refer to page 28.

Remember, love attracts more love. Show each other love in big and small ways every day! Build on the love you already share by deepening your friendship and your open communication about money with these additional reflection questions:

1. Which exercises were the most helpful – individually and as a couple?

191

2. What are you most excited to focus on now?

3. Have you filled out your Money Personality Type survey? Do you know what your primary and secondary types are? Do you know your partner's?

4. What are your limiting beliefs about money and how are you planning to shift them toward abundance? Use one of the following techniques: "Review, Reveal, and Reverse," or "Explain and Justify" or both.

5. What are you and your partner most passionate about? How can you both devote more attention and time to the things that delight your heart?

FINAL THOUGHTS:

- Remember to discuss your individual and mutual dreams on a regular basis. Dream, then dream bigger!

- Money is linked to emotions. Take time to consider each other's feelings as you move forward in your communication. Consider what may have triggered your partner. Ask questions. Be curious instead of furious.

- Remember the Magic Salt Pill story! Listen to your partner. Express your feelings and point of view as well. Remind each other of your backgrounds and history. This helps you understand each other.

- Conflicts are not inherently bad. The magic is in your ability to communicate, learn, grow and find creative solutions together.

- Celebrate each step! Celebrate each other!

Congratulations for completing this book! You have the information, insight and tools to achieve your shared vision. Now the real adventure begins! One small step at a time. Hand in hand! Heart to heart! Dollar upon dollar! You are ready to create, experience and enjoy INFINITE LOVE AND MONEY!

We believe in you!

Mollie and Joel

P.S. For more support, go to:
https://www.salaurmor.com/ and http://www.molliesingh.com/ and sign up for your *free* 30–minute sessions with us!

Appendix

APPENDIX 1

–Money Personality Types –

Instructions

ASSESSMENT: See Chapter 2 for The Money Personality Types

S stands for The Splurger Type

U stands for The Unconscious Type

G stands for The Greedy Type

A stands for The Accumulator Type

P stands for The Protectionist Type

I stands for The Investor Type

E stands for The Egotist Type

Write in column 1, a "Y" if you agree or "N" if you disagree.

1	2	3	4	5
YOUR ANSWER				YOUR COUNT
	Adjectives		# of Ss	
	addictive	S,U	# of Us	O
	adventurous	S,G	# of Gs	1
	analytical	A,P,I	# of As	

		angry	G,E	# of Ps	
		Anxious	U,G	# of Is	
		authentic	A,I	# of Es	◯
		careless	S,U,E		
		compassionate	A,P,I		
		controlling	G,A,E		
		creative	U		
		critical	G,E		
		decisive	A,I,E		
		detached	S,U,E		
		detail oriented	A,P,I		
		direct, forceful	G,E		
		disciplined	A,P,I		
		feels powerless	U,P		
		financially dependent	S,U		
		financially irresponsible	S,U,E		

	Financially successful	A,I		
	friendly	S,I	S	1
	frightened	U,G		
	frozen by fear, worry, depression	U		
	fun–loving	S	S	
	goal–oriented	(A,P,I)		
	happy–go–lucky	S,I		
	hard–working	(A,P,I)		
	highly emotional	S,G,P,E		
	impatient	S,G,E		
	impulsive	(S,G)		
	intolerant of others	G,E		
	internally motivated	A,P,I		
	lives for today	(S,G)		
	lives in the past	U,P		
	low self–control	S,E		

	manipulative	G,E		
	materialistic	S,G		
	naïve	U		
	nonconfrontational	U,P		
	obsessive	G,P,E		
	oppressive	G,E		
	planner	A,P,I		
	popular	S,I		
	powerful	I,E		
	precise	A,I		
	prone to blame	G,E		
	quiet	P		
	represses feelings and beliefs	S,U,P		
	rescuer	A,P,I		
	seeks security	A,P,I		
	self-reliant	U		

9 - S
8 - U
10 - I

	sensitive	P		
	serious	A,P		
	spiritual	U,A,I		
	supportive of others	S,A,I		
	trusting	U		
	unattached	S,U		
	undisciplined	S,U,G,E		
	uneasy	U,G		
	unforgiving	G,P,E		
	unsupported	A,I,E		

INSTRUCTIONS TO ASSESS

1. When reviewing your Y/N column –ignore all N's.

2. Now, add up all the Ss, Us, Gs, As, Ps, Is, and Es.

3. The one with the largest amount is your primary money personality type—right now. The one with the 2nd most is your secondary money personality type (you may have a tertiary money personality type if the 3rd highest amount is close to the 2nd most)—right now.

4. We say "right now," because humans are ever changing. And

199

this assessment is static. You may find different results in the coming weeks or months.

5. We recommend you do this calculation again one month from today (and again three months from today) since your money personality type can change as you make changes in your life.

APPENDIX 2

–Summary of the Money Personality Types–

	Mindset	Attitude	Action Steps	Benefits	Our Proposal
The Splurger Type	Thoughts of Entitlement	One of Desperation	Swayed easily; cost is inconsequential	They believe money comes easily and frequently.	Plan for a monthly splurge. Splurge within your means.
The Unconscious Type	Poverty mindset. They are afraid of what they might find, so they don't look.	They don't want to deal with the consequences of what they find.	No action steps!	They protect their feelings, —sadness, overwhelm, or anger— which do not serve them.	Acknowledge you are this type and start a conscious savings plan.
The Greedy Type	They have a poverty mindset. They are scared to do without.	They are hoarders. No matter how much investment return they make, they expect more.	They negotiate harshly: they have to win at all costs	Greed is an intense desire. It is this intense desire for money, that helps them acquire it.	Focus on other desires, like your relationship. That balance will be helpful for your relationship and your well–being.

	Mindset	Attitude	Action Steps	Benefits	Our Proposal
The Accumulator Type	Their safety and security is paramount. They have a worry mindset.	Negative: they are always prepared for the inevitable doomsday.	They include their partner in all money decisions—making their partner feel safe and secure; save their money for a rainy day.	They save their money. When an emergency comes up, they will have plenty to cover those expenses.	Think about ways you can share with others: Do you have a favorite charity? Act like The Splurger Type once a month!
The Protectionist Type	Protect money—at all times; in a constant state of worry.	They are afraid of the past financial crashes; something can go terribly wrong with their money at any time.	Money is in cash. They are quick to say no to all financial decisions.	Has a low likelihood of ever losing money—except to inflation.	Think about ways you can share with others: Act like The Splurger Type!

APPENDIX 3

–WAYS TO SAVE AND INVEST–

WAYS TO INVEST AND SAVE	Early 2021 yield or return	Risk(s)
Checking Account	Less than 0.1%	Inflation
Savings account	Less than 0.2%	Inflation
Certificates of Deposit (CDs)	1–year: less than 0.7% 5–year: less than 1.25%	Inflation; You invest in a 5–year CD and interest jump in the next 1–4 years and you lose out on potentially investing in much higher rates
Money Market Funds (Money Funds)	Less than 0.75%	Inflation; not guaranteed by the FDIC (Federal Deposit Investment Corporation)
Treasury bills (T–bills) Treasury Notes (T–notes) Treasury Bonds (T–Bonds)	Less than 0.1% Less than 0.5% Less than 1.85%	Inflation; no Treasury instruments are guaranteed by the government though if they did not pay their obligations, they would get downgraded and the view of the U.S. Government would be severely impaired.
Universal, Whole Life Insurance	Less than 5%	No access to your money without borrowing the funds. Surrender charge and penalties apply if you need the money soon after you invest. Return much lower in early years of policy.

WAYS TO INVEST AND SAVE	Early 2021 yield or return	Risk(s)
Variable Universal Life	Return tied to underlying fund you invest in.	You pick a poor fund. Minimum guarantee is very low—recently less than 1%.
Fixed Annuities	Less than 3.5%	Inflation. Surrender penalty if you want your money before the term ends (usually 5–7 years).
Variable Annuities	Return tied to underlying fund you invest in.	You pick a poor fund. Minimum guarantee is very low—recently less than 1%.
Corporate Bonds	Less than 3% except for the most risky companies	Credit risk—risk of company going bankrupt; inflation
Real Estate	Residential return was about 4% over the last 20 years. Commercial real estate return has been more than 8% over the last 20 years.	Illiquid: if you have to sell quickly, you will have to significantly discount the property.
Stocks	Dividend yield on S&P 500 is 1.6%; Capital gain potential much larger; 2020 return for S&P 500 was 16.3%; last 20 years was approximately 10%	You pick poor returning stocks.

APPENDIX 4

–The Budget Game–

It is my desire to keep my promise regarding all of these financial obligations and in some cases, I will even do twice as much as required

	Montly expense	O/$ Balance
Mortgage	2,100	510,000
Property Taxes	1,667	N/A
Travel	667	N/A
Kids Summer Camps	500	N/A
Daughter's voice lessons	400	N/A
Continuing Ed/ Seminars	208	N/A
Food Shopping	200	N/A
Home Equity Loan	200	100,000
Con-ED (Heat/AC)	200	N/A
Gas	200	N/A
Dinners	200	N/A

Lunches	176	N/A
Wireless phone	155	N/A
Kid's Tennis	133	N/A
Gifts for Kids	125	N/A
Professional Memberships	121	N/A
Commuter Train	100	N/A
Broadway Shows	100	N/A
Cable	85	N/A
Water	85	N/A
Snacks/Sodas	64	N/A
Books	50	N/A
Ice Creams	32	N/A
Credit Card Balances	30	N/A
Personal Loans	-	N/A
TOTAL	8,798	610,000

APPENDIX 5

–Joel's Financial Freedom Survey–

1. What is your financial freedom number?
   - ○ Under $250,000
   - ○ 250,001-500,000
   - ○ 500,001–1,000,000
   - ○ 1,000,001–2,500,000
   - ○ 2,500,001–5,000,000
   - ○ 5,000,001–10,000,000
   - ○ 10,000,001–25,000,000
   - ○ over 25,000,000

2. How did you calculate your financial freedom number?
   - ○ I guessed
   - ○ I calculated based on my current expenses
   - ○ I calculated based on my dream expenses
   - ○ Other (please specify)

   ┌───┐
   │   │
   │   │
   └───┘

3. You have achieved financial freedom. What would be your highest priority?
   - ○ Fund your children's college education
   - ○ Take a dream vacation
   - ○ Make Investments
   - ○ Buy your dream car or house
   - ○ Donate to Charities

○ Other (please specify)

4. In your childhood, you remember your parents as:

☐ Savers

☐ Spenders

☐ A bit of both

5. In your childhood, you remember your parents as:

☐ Shrewd investors

☐ Noninvestors

☐ Terrible investors

6. In your childhood, you remember money:

☐ Coming in easily

☐ Was a struggle

☐ Was a source of joy

☐ Was a source of arguments

7. Would you consider yourself:

☐ A risk taker

☐ A risk avoider

☐ Conservative

☐ Aggressive

8. Do you believe:

○ Your mindset is set for success

○ You are worthy of massive wealth

○ Neither

9. Do you believe:

☐ Your inside world impacts your outside world

☐ You should save your money for a rainy day

☐ You should not save your money for a rainy day

10. Which of the following do you believe is true?

☐ Money is the root of all evil

☐ You can't be spiritual and rich

☐ Money is not for people like us

☐ You have to work hard to make money

☐ None of the above

11. Which of the following do you believe to be true?

☐ Rich people are criminals

☐ There is never enough

☐ The rich get richer and the poor get poorer

☐ Not everyone can get rich

☐ None of the above

12. Please provide some demographic information:

○ Male

○ Female

13. Please provide your age:

○ 18–24

○ 25–39

○ 40–49

○ 50–64

○ 65–74

○ 74+

14. Household income:

- ○ Under $25,000
- ○ $25,000–$49,999
- ○ $50,000–$99,999
- ○ $100,000–$249,999
- ○ $250,000–$499,999
- ○ $500,000+

15. Net worth (assets less any debt or other liabilities including mortgage or credit card debt)

- ○ Negative $100,000 or lower
- ○ Negative $25,000–$100,000
- ○ Negative $1–$24,999
- ○ Positive but under $10,000
- ○ $10,000–$49,999
- ○ $50,000–$99,999
- ○ $100,000–$249,999
- ○ $250,000–$499,999
- ○ $500,000–$999,999
- ○ $1,000,000–$2,499,999
- ○ $2,500,000 or $5,000,000
- ○ $5,000,000 or more

16. Please provide your email address:

```
┌────────────────────────────────────────┐
│                                          │
│                                          │
│                                          │
└────────────────────────────────────────┘
```

About the Authors

Mollie Singh is an empathetic entrepreneur, university professor, mentor, Project Manager, community organizer, and author. She earned her MBA in global business and has created businesses to educate, invigorate, and enhance the community and create interpersonal growth through the arts. She is currently pursuing her doctorate in Organizational Change and Leadership. She has served on community boards as member and Organizer, and mentored individuals in their personal and professional goals. She became a Certified Infinite Possibilities Trainer and Trailblazer in 2017. When she became a Gottman 7 Principles Leader in 2018, she was inspired to connect couples spiritually and infinitely. She enjoys mentoring individuals, couples and business professionals by helping them to lead and live with intentionally, by designing and living their best lives with love. She has authored two other books, Lessons Learned From My Rescue Dog, a book as much about her beloved rescue dog as about finding her love, and Infinitely Loving, A Workbook to Support Couples In Creating a Life of Love together. Both are available on Amazon. For more information about Mollie and her services, please visit: https://www.MollieSingh.com/

Joel Salomon is a Finance and Mindful Money Expert and Master Prosperity Coach who helps others overcome obstacles standing in the way of their financial freedom. He's an award – winning speaker, workshop facilitator and frequent television and podcast guest who has been quoted in the Wall Street Journal, Newsday, U.S. News and World Report, and interviewed in Forbes and on Bloomberg Radio. As manager of a $700 million portfolio, the creator of his own successful hedge fund and the author of two best–selling books: The 9 Money Rules Millionaires Use and Mindful Money Management, Joel is an expert in the field of finance and the mindset of money. Just as he teaches in his books and seminars, the true foundation of wealth and financial freedom is a mindset of abundance, self–worth, gratitude, love and service. Becoming a Certified Infinite Possibilities Trainer and Trailblazer in 2017, ignited a dream in Joel's heart to help over 100,000 people become financially free so they too, could live the life of their dreams. He's well on his way to making that dream a reality! For more information about Joel and his services, please visit: https://www.salaurmor.com/

Made in the USA
Middletown, DE
28 June 2021